Counting My Blessings

Gill & Macmillan
Hume Avenue, Park West, Dublin 12
www.gillmacmillanbooks.ie

978 0 7171 6878 1

Design by Fidelma Slattery
Edited by Alison Walsh
Printed and bound by CPI Group (UK) Ltd, Croydon, CRO 4YY

This book is typeset in Linux Libertine and Saint Agnes.

The paper used in this book comes from the wood pulp of managed
forests. For every tree felled, at least one tree is planted, thereby
renewing natural resources.

A CIP catalogue record for this book is available from the British Library.

5 4 3 2 1

Counting My Blessings

Francis Brennan's Guide to HAPPINESS

GILL & MACMILLAN

CONTENTS

INTRODUCTION

As you might know, in 2014 I wrote a book about etiquette called *It's The Little Things*. I enjoyed it so much, and getting out and about all over the country to talk to people, that I decided to write another! I thought long and hard about what to write about. I'd wanted to tell my story for a long time, but wasn't sure how – I didn't want to drone on with 'Then I did this and then I did that' like a bore at a party. And besides, no one can ever be truly accurate about his or her own life. As Herbert Samuel said: 'An autobiography is the story of how a man thinks he lived.'

And then I met a man in Pittsburgh and it all fell into place.

I do an annual tour of the US for Tourism Ireland and off I went in February 2015, ending up in Pittsburgh during the big freeze when it snowed for weeks and temperatures plummeted. On this particular day it was minus 23 degrees

Fahrenheit. That's minus 30 degrees Celsius, just so you know! Now, I had to do some printing and so I walked the few blocks to where the nice lady in the hotel had told me I could find a copy store. Of course, there was hardly a soul about; the only people out on the street were 'street bums', as they call them, who all let a roar at me as I walked by, God help them.

I needed 200 copies of a brochure and so I left it in and said I'd be back later to collect it. I was half-distracted on the walk there and back, as I was thinking about the rehearsal for a Tourism Ireland show we were doing that night, so when I went out later to pick the printing up, I got lost. I wandered up and down a bit, but all of the buildings looked the same and I couldn't get my bearings. Then I saw a gentleman coming towards me and I said, 'Excuse me, sir. Is there a print shop here?'

He looked perfectly normal, wrapped up against the cold, and he was very pleasant. 'Oh, yes,' he said. 'But you're at the back door. The front door is one block back. But wait here; I'm just going in.'

I waited, and he let me in the back door to a little lobby which led into the shop. The copy shop woman obviously knew him because she said, 'Hello, Thomas. I'll just get your stuff now.'

We started to chat and he said, 'I'm a retired army veteran and I do some fundraising. What about you?' I told him that I was in the hotel and tourism business. We chatted about how you wouldn't be thinking about a holiday now because it's so cold – chitchat really – and then he happened to mention that he had a son in Afghanistan and he worried about him all the time. He talked more about the fundraising he did for the veterans because they needed so much money. He explained that he sold tickets to basketball and football games and so on, and made a little bit of a profit for veterans' charities.

I said, 'Sure you're very good and you do marvellous work, so let me give you something to put into the kitty,' and I gave him a $10 bill. He thanked me and we chatted a bit more until my brochures were ready. I was about to leave when the gentleman came over to me and gave me the biggest hug I've ever had from anybody – and then he whispered in my ear: 'I have to tell you the truth. I'm a street bum and I don't do any fundraising at all. I just keep the money, but do you know what? You are the first person in five years who has treated me as an equal, so my conscience wouldn't let me not tell you the truth.'

He then proceeded to tell me his story: a divorce had lost him everything and he became homeless; five years later, he was still living on the street. He just needed to get a step up, he explained. Then he tried to give me back the $10. I said, 'No, no. Take the $10 and from today on you'll think of the strength you had to tell me the truth because that wasn't easy for you. Just go forward from here. Today's the day it's all going to change.' And then I got my printing and he got his, and we went our separate ways. Who knows where this man is now or what he's doing, but I hope he has been able to get that step up in life that he needed.

I'm not telling you this story to show you all what a great man I am, but simply to say that life can deal us any kind of a hand, good or bad. Often it's a bit of both, and the only difference is what we make of it. And that's the subject of this book – how we handle what life throws at us and learn to make the most of it. In short, it's a book about happiness.

Nowadays, we are inundated with advice about happiness. You only have to open a book or a magazine to see an article about how to be happy – 'Ten tips to a happier life', all that kind of thing. It seems that happiness can be hard to find these days! And yet I often wonder if it's because we expect too much; we expect to be jumping for joy all the time and life to be one big load of fun. But we all know that life isn't like that – that it has its ups and downs and its challenges and somehow we just have to get through them. Maybe this isn't a very glamorous notion, but it's the truth.

Needless to say, I don't think I'm an expert on the subject of happiness, but I am a happy person. Maybe it's because I'm fortunate enough to have been born that way, but maybe it's also because of my philosophy on life. I am someone who has always gotten on with whatever life has given me, good and bad. I've always felt that happiness is something you choose, rather than it choosing you. Now, I can almost hear you say, 'That's all very well for you, Francis, with your TV show and your hotel and all the travel. Sure, you have a great life altogether.' Well, nobody's life is perfect, and mine is no more perfect than anybody else's. I've had great opportunities in life and I look on them as a blessing, but I've also worked hard every single day and I've earned every penny I have. Like many others, the recession wasn't kind to me, but it's all relative and I've taken responsibility for my own mistakes. Meeting my challenges has helped me to keep going and come out the other side. I'm still happy, because I believe in that quote I found while I was thinking about this book: 'Being happy doesn't mean that everything is perfect. It just means that you've decided to look beyond the imperfections.'

I've been lucky enough to have wonderful parents who were role models and to have grown up in a happy family. Without that, and my parents' positive attitude, maybe I wouldn't look at life in the way I do. I was born with a deformity in my right foot and had eleven major operations when

I was a child. My parents did everything for me and ensured I had the best of care, but it was their attitude that made all the difference. They encouraged me to just get on with life and not to let it hold me back. And so it hasn't. My work ethic I inherited from my dad, who worked long hours at our family shop in Stepaside, Co. Dublin. I also get a lot from the things that make me happy in life – work, travel, my faith, my family – and I'm going to share these with you in this book. Most important, I've never underestimated the power of making other people happy.

But what about me, I hear you say. How can I be happy? Well, when writing this book, I started thinking about all the things that contribute to happiness in my life. Take a look – I hope that they can help to make your life a little happier too.

– Gratitude –

I know it may be difficult when things are tough, but simply counting your blessings and appreciating what's around you can make you feel a lot happier. I've certainly found this to be the case in recent times. I try to appreciate my nieces and nephews, my brothers and sisters, my work, my faith, my garden in Kenmare – all the things that matter to me; I even try to appreciate and enjoy my travels around the country for *At Your Service*! So, if you can, just stop for a moment every day and take in your surroundings; maybe there's a tree that's coming into leaf, or water rushing over stones, or a warm breeze. Try it – just spend some time 'noticing', rather than rushing and worrying, and see what happens. And if you start to notice then you'll gradually come to appreciate the simple things in life.

– Positivity –

Do you remember that book *The Power of Positive Thinking*? It was written a by a man called Norman Vincent Peale and it was actually published during the 1950s, when the world was a very different place. He thought that there was only one way to look at life – by focusing on positivity – but this doesn't mean pretending that the world is a fantastic place altogether and, sure, we don't have a problem in the world. It's about accepting the realities of our lives, but trying, if we possibly can, to focus on the good bits, even if they are only little things. Now you might say, Well, Francis, I've lost my job or my cat's just died – I'm not feeling too cheerful right now. Of course you're not, but maybe your son or daughter has done well in school or your best friend's coming home from Australia for a visit – there's always something to enjoy and appreciate, even if it's just something small.

– Resilience –

I think the recession has shown us how resilient we can all be. We've been able to find our way through the tough times and are ready to 'bounce back' when things improve. I've certainly found that to be the case and have made no secret of my ups and downs in recent years. We all know that life isn't perfect, but the good news is that with some practice we can all learn to be more resilient. We all know about 'glass half full' and 'glass half empty' people. Well, apparently, research has shown that realism is best. I suppose you could say that realistic people are those who accept that their glass is at the half-way point, but feel optimistic that it'll be re-filled before long. I'll be honest with you that I've come to find that in my own life, but I've tried to accept my responsibility to myself, and responsibility for myself, and to face up to my difficulties.

– Connecting –

'No man is an island'; we need to connect with other human beings, even in small ways. I'm lucky enough to have a great family, but even so I find that, as a single person with no children, making that connection with others is particularly important in my life; be it getting into conversation while I'm waiting in line or saying hello to my neighbour – it makes me feel part of the world.

– Giving –

It may seem funny to say that giving makes us feel happier. What about receiving, I hear you say, that's nice too! But, believe me, giving will make you feel ten times happier. I try to give every day, and I don't mean a big contribution to charity or anything like that; I mean just a tip to a waiter or my best thank you to the girl in the shop. The little things really add up, I find.

– Setting goals –

It can be really worthwhile to set a goal or two in life, and to work to achieve that. A few years ago, a friend asked me to write my retirement plans on a piece of paper. I'll tell you what these were later in the book (you'll have to wait!), but I can honestly say that it did me the world of good to ask myself what I really wanted out of life. The key is to make your goals realistic for you. Say you've always wanted to write. Start by writing a short story or by joining a creative writing group, rather than leaping straight into your own *War and Peace*!

– Continually learning –

As we get older, it can be tempting to put on the slippers and sit in front of *Fair City* every night. After all, we have nothing left to learn, have we? Well, statistics show that people who continue to learn through life are much happier than those who don't. I have to say, I found my first few outings on television pretty nerve-wracking, but I'm so pleased that I dug in and got on with it. 'Feel the fear and do it anyway' is my motto! And, as far as I'm concerned, learning needn't mean taking on a PhD or skydiving; it can simply mean trying out that Spanish class you've been meaning to look into, or learning to cook Chinese food, or joining a book club. Anything that keeps your outlook on life fresh can't be bad!

– Working within our limitations –

When we're young, we all think we're going to be brain surgeons or rocket scientists, but as we grow we are faced with our own limitations as human beings. It can be an awful disappointment to realise that we'll never don a Munster jersey or fill Carnegie Hall, but part of being happy is accepting ourselves and working with what we have. In school, I wasn't a high achiever academically and my wonky foot meant that I'd never be captain of the rugby team, but instead of being sorry that I couldn't take Leinster to the Heineken Cup finals I focused on my other skills and talents, such as my business brain, and developed those.

– Believing –

I find meaning in life through my faith and through meetings with other people, like my friend in Pittsburgh, which really do make me happy. What gives your life meaning? Make a note of it and try to remember it every day.

So there we have it – my ideas on what makes us happy. I'm not perfect, of course – who is? But I'm grateful to have the attitude to life that I do, because I think this can make all the difference. I'm happy to be happy!

1.
Family
Matters

*'Folks are usually about as happy as they
make up their minds to be.'*
Abraham Lincoln

When I was in the US on my tourism trip in 2015, I went to mass, as I do regularly, in a church in New York. The priest gave a forty-minute sermon. I have to say I'd never sat through a forty-minute sermon before, but this priest, who was from Jamaica, was fascinating on the subject of fatherhood and it chimed with me because I'd been giving a lot of thought to fathers for this book. He explained that he was one of nine children and he never had a father. His father had simply left the family, leaving his mother to raise all nine children single-handed.

When he joined the priesthood, he had a psychiatric evaluation and of course the psychiatrist insisted, 'You must have a feeling of absence because you don't have a father.'

He was adamant that he didn't. 'My mother looked after us – she worked three jobs to provide for us – but we also had a community around us. And if Mum wasn't around Granny looked after us, and if Granny wasn't around Aunty Joan would look after us and her husband would play ball with us. Don't put me into the box of being odd because I have no father.' For this priest, what made up for the absence of his father was a strong mother, an involved extended family and a good community.

Now, unlike this priest, I was lucky enough to have a great dad in Tom Brennan, a shopkeeper from Milltown in Dublin. According to George Eliot in *Middlemarch*, 'It's a father's duty to give his sons a fine chance.' I suppose that was a father's role in those days – to set up his sons (and daughters) in life, and to provide them with an education.

I was fortunate enough that my father did give me 'a fine chance' in so many ways, and that he was very much a part of my life growing up since I worked with him from the age of eight or nine. I credit my dad with so much and I can see how much of myself I get from him; I have many of my father's genes, I can see that.

When I think of Dad, I often think of that song by Mike and the Mechanics, 'The Living Years', which is about a father seeing his own father in his new-born son's features. It's a beautiful song and I think the sentiment is so apt. The song also stresses the importance of communication between the generations. Today, fathers have such an important role to play in their children's lives. I see my brother John with his children and they are always talking and doing things together. But in my day it was different. For a start, we rarely saw Dad at home. My dad worked every single day from 7.00 a.m. to 7.00 p.m., and since he was caught up with the business any chat we did have was business chat: the VAT man was driving him mad, that kind of thing. He'd come in after the nine o'clock news, have a cup of tea and a biscuit, watch the telly and then go to bed. Then he was gone when we woke up in the morning. Because of the business, we never really holidayed together; we never had conversations about sport or anything else (mind you, none of us was sporty!); and we never 'talked' in the way I see families talking nowadays, when anything goes.

I have to say, when people go on and on about the 'good old days', when life was simpler and so much nicer, they seem to forget that it was a lot harder too! Sure, why wouldn't we be happy nowadays when we have Mum and Dad to talk to, and when we can be so much more open than previous generations? Maybe that's why a recent survey I came across in a US magazine stated that parents rated their happiness as 17 per cent higher than when they were children. Communication is the key to happiness, I think!

I do have one particular memory of my father, when he 'rescued' my older brother Damien and me from The Big Fog, as we always called it, in 1963 or so. We'd gotten the number 44 bus home from school as usual, but we'd hardly left the city when we had to get off because the fog was so thick. En masse, we walked up Harcourt Street, and Damien and I glued ourselves to the group for fear we'd get lost. Now, I wasn't a bit happy about walking up Harcourt Street because I'd read all about a notorious murder that had happened on this street that year. It was called the Green Tureen murder because the murderer, a student in the Royal College of Surgeons, had disposed of his girlfriend's remains in the ovens of the restaurant where he worked, the Green Tureen. The story had gripped the city because it was so grisly and because, at the time, that kind of thing was unheard of in Ireland. Our little band of Dubliners walked and walked until, as we were crossing the Dodder at Milltown, Dad appeared out of the mist. I can still remember him grabbing us both and hugging us as if he'd thought we were lost for ever. He'd been out looking for us all afternoon.

As I said, I would have seen more of my father than most because, by the time I was eight or nine years old, I was working with him in the family business. My father gave me the best work ethic anyone could have, in the same way as his father had instilled a work ethic in him, even though my dad had had to pull himself up by the bootstraps, as the saying goes. I know that, at one stage, my father's family were prosperous. Dad's father, Paul, was on the Board of Works and had bought a row of houses in

Milltown called The Colonnade. The family business was, and still is, Christmas trees, although Dad's father would have had a number of other businesses as well. Dad's father was a very cultured man and a great friend of Count John McCormack. Apparently he used to accompany the Count on tour in Ireland, and I can imagine that that would have been something else, as they say! Of course, we never really do appreciate our family history, do we? Which reminds me of a funny story. Dad's father had all of Count John McCormack's records at home, old 78s, signed of course. When he died very suddenly of some kind of pulmonary disease at forty-two years of age, my father was only four-teen. One day, he and his brother decided to amuse themselves by playing Frisbee with the records, throwing them out of the window at the garden wall so they could hear that distinctive 'crack' they made, because, of course, they were all made out of shellac. Can you imagine? Needless to say, my dad was mortified when he realised not only their value, but their importance.

Following Granddad's death, the family was in an ab-solute state, both emotionally and financially, with death duties and everything else. My father was taken out of school in CUS (Catholic University School), where I would later go to school, and set to work in the family business. The houses in The Colonnade had to be sold off. (The family gradually bought the houses in The Colonnade back. In a nice little aside, when they were listed the Christmas lights that were up on them at the time were included – so the family now has to keep the lighted-up Santa and Happy Christmas on the houses all year round! They're a bit of a Milltown landmark.)

My father gradually built up a business, starting with a grocers in Milltown known as The Bridge Stores, and then he expanded and built a store in Stepaside. At the time, Stepaside was in the countryside and he saw an opening there, supplying groceries to people who were too far away from shops and the new supermarkets that were opening up all over the place. My father's Stepaside shop was, in fact, one of Ireland's first supermarkets. My father should have started something like Superquinn because he had the foresight and the knowledge to see that that's where shopping was going. He had lots of facilities in his shop that were unheard of at the time, such as toilets and sinks, and was up to speed on hygiene before anyone. He also had a slicing machine with a blade that detached so you could wash it. And if you left a crumb on it, he'd eat you. My father had very high standards.

It was never really discussed, but I found that I naturally gravitated towards the Stepaside shop. I learned a lot about Dad, working with him. He could be a perfectionist and the shop was always immaculate, with a place for everything and everything in its place. I was reminded of Dad when I was in San Francisco recently and I went to the Apple store because I had a problem with my iPhone. I was highly entertained when I was directed to the 'genius bar' to fix my iPhone! But what reminded me of Dad was that there was a girl by the elevator fixing boxes so that they lined up nicely and I said to her, 'Now, do it right, because my father used to make me do that, and if there was a tin of beans off centre, he'd eat you.' Now, needless to say, my father never once hit me or used corporal punishment in any way, but I learned from his example how important it was to get things right. Like him, I'm a man for detail – I'll even admit that I'm a bit over the top about it – but detail matters in my business.

Dad was also totally reliable. At that time, if you lived outside the city you'd order your groceries once a week to be delivered and Tom Brennan would never let you down. We used to do deliveries in our Opel Caravan up to Ticknock, Glencullen, Glencree and all those areas in the Dublin and Wicklow mountains, in all weathers. In the time before supermarkets people often had groceries delivered like this. I remember one lady used to order the usual things – pound of butter, tea, sliced pan and so on – but at the end of every list she always had 'instant whiff'. It took me a while to work out that she meant 'instant whip' or Angel Delight!

Working in the shop and listening to Dad, I also learned a lot about the psychology of people. I learned that rich people didn't always buy the best and that poorer people would buy expensive things, maybe because they wanted to feel that they could live well even if they didn't have the money. Dad, being generous to a fault, extended credit to a lot of people. In fact, when he died, a lot of people came out of the woodwork, turning up at our door with brown envelopes addressed by hand to 'Mr Brennan'. We didn't realise it, but he'd lent money all over the place, and clearly it was on their conscience. You can imagine if that many people came forward, many more didn't. They say, 'Neither a borrower nor a lender be,' but my dad ignored the advice and, quite honestly, so did I when I had money to help other people out. I'm not saying this so you'll think, 'What a great man altogether,' but I can freely admit that I've never given money a lot of thought in that way. I don't resent it – I'm like my father in that way. Yes, I have lent money, quite a lot of it, and, no, I probably won't get it all back, but like my dad I don't harbour any resentment. What is it that they say? Giving is its own reward!

I also know that I have my dad's entrepreneurial spirit. Even from an early age, I had some kind of little business going. My first enterprise was selling lemonade from our house in Balally, near Dundrum, Co. Dublin. My brother Damien was always theatrical and we'd put on shows, arguing about when to open and close the curtains, which never worked properly. I'd sell lemonade for a penny a glass during the interval. And then, of course, there were the Christmas logs that I wrote about in *It's The Little Things*, which I got from Scout Headquarters up in Larch Hill when we'd do deliveries. I'd bring them home, split them and decorate them with Hector Grey fake snow, and Bob's your uncle – Christmas logs! Then I had my babysitting service, which went down a bomb since our little cul-de-sac of 37 houses was expanded by a full 600 during the 1960s. I coordinated the local teenagers, taking a 10 per cent cut of their earnings – I clearly remember that one night I had forty-two working for me!

I don't know whether there was a tiny bit of the ghost of Granddad hanging over us, so that I felt that somehow I had to compensate for the losses after his death by never being without money. Whatever it was, I know that having money was important to me, not because I was greedy or wanted to be rich, but because it gave me a sense of security, and I found that I had the knack for making it and enjoyed the whole business of it. I was always doing tons of things and I was always making money, right from an early age, and, honestly, I got used to it. I remember a friend saying to me once that I didn't really understand what people were going through during the crash because, 'You've always had money.' She was right, I suppose – it can be a dangerous thing. Quite honestly, when I go to buy a suit, it doesn't matter to me if it's €650 or €250 – I just buy it. Of course that's not the real world and I know that – in the real world, people have to save money for things like that – but I also know that I understand the value of money. When times were good, I never bought a helicopter or spent in that kind of way. I cannot abide waste in life. When I was in San Francisco on my latest Tourism Ireland trip, they were all hopping into taxis from the airport and paying $156 to get into town, but I thought that was daft – I hopped on the train, which got there before them! I always go a comfortable way, but I won't waste money.

I'm proud of my work ethic, which I got from my parents. In the shop, I just got on with helping Dad and I didn't get paid either. I still work ridiculously hard, not just because I have to these days – of which more later – but because I enjoy it. Work gives me such energy, and it makes me happy in the same way as a hobby or exercise would make someone else happy. This is probably fortunate, because a typical day for me at Park Hotel Kenmare is long, beginning at 8.30 a.m. every morning and going on until 11.00 p.m. or so at night. It involves checking out guests, talking to the chef about the menu, doing the post and hovering during service, as well as organising my schedule for filming *At Your Service*, along with a number of other commitments – and I love it all.

My mother, Maura, was very different from Dad. Like so many women of her generation, she gave up work when she married, having moved to Dublin from her native Sligo to join the civil service in 1947. She met Dad at a dance and married him in the Church of the Holy Name in Ranelagh in 1951. The rest of her life would be devoted to bringing up the Brennans – Damien, who was born in 1952, me (1953), another little boy called Thomas who, sadly, was stillborn, then Kate (1956), Susan (1957) and John, 'the baby', who was born in 1965, an event which I clearly remember. I recall going in to the National Maternity Hospital in Holles Street to visit the new arrival and being unable to believe that he was so small. I was terrified that Mum would break his little arms putting them into his babygro.

I remember my mother telling me a nice story about when Damien was born in 1952. My mother's father came up from Sligo to see the new arrival. As my father was bringing him back to the station to get the train, they passed the National Maternity Hospital. My father said casually, 'That's where Damien was born' and Granddad thought that Dad was a very rich man and that was his house. He was delighted his daughter had married so well!

It wouldn't be the way nowadays, I know, but I can say that my mother was the centre of our home. She was naturally a warm and sociable woman, who provided a welcome for numerous visitors from Sligo. Ours was very much an 'open house', and we'd often come home from school to find we'd been turfed out of our bedroom for a night to accommodate some visitor from home. My mother would also regularly entertain distant cousins, such as Eithne Pugh and Marie Jennings, at Sunday lunch. I think I owe my sociable nature to Mum! It's a role that my sister Kate has taken up in the family now, and I always stay with her when I'm up in Dublin.

Mum and Dad only rowed once that I know of – amazing, isn't it? It was a Sunday night and I have no idea what the row was even about, but all I know is that Mum stayed in the kitchen doing Monday's washing instead of sitting in the living room, as she did every Sunday night, eating the chocolate macaroons that Dad would buy her every week. That said a lot, because in those days the washing was a huge job that you wouldn't do before you absolutely had to. The five of us were devastated – that was the greatest catastrophe of my childhood, as far as I was concerned, which shows how stable my parents were! I count myself very lucky because I know that this gave me a firm foundation in life. Mind you, I think Mum was probably a silent worrier: Dad used to say he could have been like Fergal Quinn with a whole range of stores only for Mum because she was a cautious woman, but on the other hand she may well have prevented him from taking unnecessary risks. As we later discovered, Dad's generosity sometimes got the better of him, so maybe it was a good thing that Mum was there to apply the brakes!

My parents were a great mix of city and country and we spent many summers on my mother's family farm in Sligo. I can still remember the house: it was a thatched cottage with two rooms on the bottom and a single room on top. There was no running water. You used to wash yourself on the 'street', the yard in front of the house. I remember my grandfather shaving on that wall, bringing a kettle out of the house from the open fire. We used to go to Sligo every summer, from the first day of the school holidays to the last. My brother Damien, who is just a year older than me, loved the business of farming and haymaking, all that kind of thing, but I was more the domestic man – I'd bring the sandwiches and the tea out to the fields in a 7-pound stainless steel can, or in a Lucozade bottle because they had great sealing tops. You'd wrap the can in newspapers and pop it on the bike and off you'd go, out into the fields. My mother's brother and sister, Anna and Jim, were very good to us. When you're children you don't notice how good people are to you, but I understand now and I thank them for it. Things have now come full circle in that my brother Damien bought the farm from my aunt and lives there now, and, after many years in the tourism and restaurant business, currently runs a tour called the Yeats Experience, using his theatrical flair, which is fantastic.

My mother's early life wasn't without trauma. At age three she lost her index finger when her brother chopped it off – accidentally, I hasten to add. He was chopping logs and Mum's finger had somehow gotten in the way. My mother still remembers her father's panic as he got the horse and trap ready to take her the three miles to the local hospital. It was too late for her finger, sadly, but she adapted well, winning prizes for her handwriting, would you believe!

Mum created a very happy home life for us all. For a start, she insisted that we all eat together. As the saying goes, 'The family that eats together, stays together.' We always had the best of food. When my father died, we had little left financially and I used to joke that it was because we ate it! Our house was legendary for serving steaks, roast beef, chicken or lamb chops at a time when meat was expensive. Now, this might sound extravagant, but I think everyone decides on their priorities in life and ours was to eat well, probably because of Mum's farming background – and we're all healthy as a result.

I remember once my mother decided to buck the trend. She rang my father in the shop and announced, 'Bring down some mince because we're going to have that for dinner.' My father was horrified. 'What?' he said, unable to believe his ears. You couldn't have mince – my father would have considered that inferior. But he did what he was told and 2 pounds of mince was duly dispatched from Stepaside. Mum mixed it with onion and then dipped it in egg and breadcrumbs to make rissoles, which were then fried on the pan. We came in and sat up at the table, asking,

'What's for lunch?' With a flourish, she put them down in front of us.

When we saw the rissoles, Damien and I said simultaneously, 'Are we not having any meat?' We took our meat seriously in the Brennan household!

I now know that that our meat-eating habit ate into our profits in the shop, because, as it transpired, we weren't well off at all. We were always robbing Peter to pay Paul. That's normal in a cash-flow business, where you always seem to have money, but appearances can be deceptive, as we'd later learn. But my mother was a stickler for the family lunch, to the extent that we'd have to go home from school for lunch every day – even though it was two bus journeys away.

My mother was also a very compassionate woman, who took a great interest in others. I remember a family on our road, the Vanaceks, who were considered very exotic at the time because they'd fled the communists in what was then Czechoslovakia. They were terribly bookish and musical and their house was full of violins and other instruments. I can also clearly remember that they grew sunflowers, long before it was fashionable to do so. I used to be terrified of those sunflowers – it was like the *The Day of the Triffids* in the Vanaceks'! They'd adopted an Irish boy, Martin, a lovely boy who wasn't even slightly like his adopted parents or sister. The Vanaceks were a lovely family, but the poor fellow stood out like a sore thumb. He even found it hard to get used to European food and my mother used to smuggle him Irish stew!

Poor Martin was always in trouble and the family had to keep moving him from one school to another as he'd get into scrapes. One day, my mother was out cutting the grass when Martin came up the road. He'd just gotten off the bus and he was in a new school uniform.

'Hello, Martin. How are you?' my mother said.

'Fine, thanks, Mrs Brennan,' he replied.

'And where are you going to school now?' she said.

'I don't know. It's written on my cap.' The poor fellow no longer knew where he was going!

My mother hardly ever lost her temper; she governed with a kind of strict compassion, for want of a better expression, but we knew where we stood with her. Only once do I remember her ever losing her temper with me. I couldn't have been more than five or six years of age, and we were getting ready to go on a picnic to Donabate. Dad would close the shop for a half day, which you did in the days before 24-hour opening, and Mum would prepare a picnic, and we'd set off then to our family friends, the Redmonds, who used a converted railway carriage as a beach home in Donabate. My mother had warned me several times not to pick the lovely white roses that grew in our back garden, but, undeterred, I somehow managed to pluck the heads off them all, passing the kitchen window with my hands, stuffed with flower heads, behind my back. There was murder when she found out what I'd done and there was no outing to Donabate that day. Plus I got a clip on the ear for my troubles. My mother never, ever disciplined us like that and she often says now that she regrets her overreaction – but I've forgiven her!

My mother is ninety-three now and of course we're all grown up. Kate was a medical secretary for many years, to one of the country's foremost Down Syndrome specialists and more recently to the President of the Royal College of Surgeons of Ireland; Susan is a chartered physiotherapist, and when we were all living at home we used to be highly entertained by the number of her suitors, medical students all, who'd turn up at the door in sports cars. Mum is still very much the matriarch, keeping us all posted on what the others are doing and giving out a bit! She still lives in Sligo and we take it in turns to visit her and keep an eye on things, even though only Damien and Susan live there now. And if I don't do my bit one of my sisters will be on the phone to me!

Just before my visit to the US in spring 2015, my sister Kate rang me to see if I'd be dropping up to Mum before I left. Between ourselves, I hadn't planned a visit, as I had three board meetings in Dublin and a plane to catch, but Kate let me know that it'd be noticed, so off I went up to Sligo.

'Now, Mum,' I said, when I arrived. 'Have you a list of the things that need doing?'

'Oh, yes,' she replied. 'I need to visit the chiropodist and have my hair done.'

So off we went into Sligo town and I parked outside the chiropodist's. It's a very narrow street, so I had to park half on the pavement, my flashers on. Out I got and held the door open for Mum. She climbed out of the car and, while she did so, I heard her push the button down; as I closed the door, it dawned on me that the keys were still inside. Uh-oh, I thought, as I led her inside, promising her that I'd be back in an hour after I'd gone for a 'little walk to pass the time'. I ran back outside to find a queue of cars waiting to pass mine, and I had to stand in the middle of the road directing traffic! Half the town passed me, waving away, as I stood there. I then had to ring around half the garages in the West of Ireland before I found a lovely local man, who was only too glad to come along with his special machine for opening my window just enough to push a coat hanger down – the old methods are still the best! – and pull the keys out. And you know what? I made it back into the chiropodist's to my mother an hour later, not a bother.

'Did you have a nice walk?' she asked.

'Perfect, Mum,' I answered, 'Just perfect.' She didn't need to know!

Now, I love telling stories about Mum, and one of my favourites is a driving one. My mother only learned to drive in her sixties, after Dad died. It may seem strange nowadays, but in her day many women left the driving to their husbands. However, as Mum lived in the country and was now alone, she needed to learn. And so she did. She wasn't afraid to learn new things, even in later life.

She needed a smaller car than the large saloon that Dad had driven, and so we acquired a Morris Minor from an opera singer in Dromahair. This lady was returning to the US and needed to sell her black Morris Minor, which we thought would be just perfect – not too big for Mum. I can still remember the number plate, RIP 144, which was unfortunate...

Along with the Morris Minor, Mum had also acquired two nuns – two long-lost cousins who had come back from the US for the summer and were visiting her in Sligo. They were from the Katharine Drexel order, and I remember that they taught Native American students in New Orleans. It was the very first time they'd been allowed to return to their native Ireland since they'd joined the order. I can still remember that they wore a very large and elaborate wimple with a kind of white square box on their heads – they were quite a sight, sitting up in the back of the Morris Minor (Mum decided to put them in the back of the car, as it was safer)!

Off they went into Sligo town to the supermarket one day. Mum had to negotiate the car park for the first time, and as she pulled into a parking space the car in the space in front pulled out. Oh, great, she thought, if I pull forward I won't have to reverse out. She hadn't noticed the raised pedestrian walkway in between the parking spaces, which was marked with a little concrete wall and a small bollard. So, as she accelerated forward, she hit the kerb and up the car shot and landed on the bollard. 'Don't move!' she ordered the nuns, as the car wobbled around on the bollard. She didn't dare get out in case she unbalanced it, so she beeped the horn. Thankfully, some local workmen came to her aid, lifting the car up, with its cargo of Mum and the two nuns, and putting it gently back down on the ground, even managing to place it dead centre in the parking space.

Life changed for the Brennans when Dad became ill with emphysema. Like so many men of his generation, he smoked like a trooper. He was only fifty-three and Mum was still in her forties, which, now that I look back on it, was very hard on her. At that stage, just after I'd left secondary school, Mum and Dad had left Dublin and moved back to Sligo, where they had a plan to build a guesthouse on a lovely site overlooking Lough Gill, Ben Bulben and Beezie's Island, so called after its last inhabitant, a lady called Beezie who lived there until 1948. It would have been just glorious, but it wasn't to be, sadly, as the bank didn't give them the money – in those days banks were very conservative about that kind of thing. However, I do credit my parents' plans for forming the idea in my mind of going into the hotel business, though my father's 'taily coat', as I called it when I was a child, also played a part. This was a tail-coat like the one Fred Astaire used to wear that Dad had bought in Louis Copeland. I used to dress up in it and pretend to receive guests. I remember thinking that it'd be great if my parents built a guesthouse because I could wear the taily coat and position myself in the front hall like a concierge, directing operations.

Even though my parents never did build that guesthouse, they built a wooden frame house in Sligo on a site they'd bought adjacent to Mum's family farm. By that stage, Dad's emphysema had taken a toll. Even though Mum found it hard to settle back into Sligo, because so many of her old friends had left, it was much easier for Dad to live there, because when he went to get the paper he could park the car in the middle of the street and nobody minded. He was slow to do things and it'd take him a long time to get in and out of the car. Moving to Sligo, where the pace of life was slower, prolonged his life hugely.

Mind you, the slower pace took a little getting used to after all those years of rushing in Dublin. In Dublin they used to get up at 7.30 a.m. to get ready for the day, but by the time they moved to Sligo Damien was in Maynooth studying for the priesthood, I was working and the girls were in boarding school in Arklow; there was only John, the baby, left and he just had to walk around the corner to school, so they could get up at 8.45 a.m. Mum used to wonder about all of those lost hours and years rushing around! She often says that she wishes they'd gone to Sligo years before, which is sad in some ways.

Even though the rest of us had left home, Mum still used to worry about John, who is dyslexic. In those days, if you were dyslexic it was simply thought that you were stupid, and there was no help at all for you. So when John went to school in Ballisodare and found that he'd be learning English, Irish, German and French, my mother used to say, 'Oh, God, he'll be illiterate in four languages.' Thankfully, John has come into his own since then, but at the time it certainly wasn't easy for him.

They say that the best-made plans often go awry, and it was no different for me. After I did my Leaving Cert, from which I emerged with a single honour (I wasn't a natural student!), I managed to get onto a training programme with Jury's Hotel in Sligo, happily enough. I can still remember that Director Peter Malone interviewed me. It was a very busy hotel and one that did a lot of functions, often for 700 guests at a time. I used to work in the kitchens and I'd lay out 700 trifles for dessert. I was happy as Larry, though, getting to and from home on the bike I'd bought for the purpose. The hotel business was all I'd ever wanted to be involved in, right from the days of my 'taily coat', and here I was at last, learning the ropes. But all that was to end in 1973, when Dad's illness became too much for him. I had to give up my traineeship and come back to Dublin because, with the others in school or away, I was the only one available to run the business and Dad wanted to keep it going for the family – not to mention the fact that we needed the money. I ran the shop for a year and a half, but when Dad offered it to me, I said no. I was mad about the hotel business and had set my heart on it. I always remember that when we sold the shop and paid everybody, there was £13,000 left. This might sound like a lot, but Dad was only fifty-three, with no pension, a wife at home and two girls in boarding school. It wasn't easy – even though the sirloin steak still continued to appear!

I didn't resent it for a minute, though, that year and a half running the shop. It was what needed to be done at the time and it happened to fall to me. And rightly so. I knew what I was doing, having spent so many years learning the ropes, and it felt good to be able to support the family and to repay my parents for everything they'd given me. And I'm a firm believer in getting on with things – I don't overanalyse or overthink; maybe that's a failing, but it allows me to get on with life. I suppose that's grit and determination for you – that resilience I mentioned in the Introduction. Learning that art will really stand you in good stead when things are difficult because you'll be able to bounce back, ready for when things improve. I also think that direction is very important – even though I was happy to help out, I always had a strong sense of where I wanted to be in life in the long run.

Dad died in 1988. I can clearly remember the phone call. I was in Vancouver at the time on a Tourism Ireland sales trip. It's a long way to come home when you're feeling down all the way. It was a difficult time for all of us.

The call didn't come as a shock to me because Dad had been ill for many years and had been close to death many times, so perhaps his passing was a relief since he had suffered terribly. No one likes to see a parent suffer. The trip home to Sligo passed in something of a blur, but my abiding memory of it was the care and attention I got from Aer Lingus staff. I know that they have protocols for dealing with bereaved families, but they were absolutely fantastic. On arrival in New York, where I was to change planes, they met me on the tarmac in a private car so I didn't have to go through the terminal. They drove me to the executive lounge and looked after me with great kindness. In Dublin Airport, the personal treatment continued: an employee escorted me from the plane through the airport, from where I headed to Sligo.

It wasn't a 'normal' funeral in that Dad had given his body to science, which meant that we only had a mass at the house, from where his body was taken to Galway University. The following day we had a church service, but no burial. This might sound strange, but Dad's memorial mass wasn't a sad event because we were happy that he was in a better place, he'd suffered so much. Looking back now, it must have been very hard for my mother as she had nursed him at home for seventeen years and now there was a big void in her life. I missed him terribly, of course, but had come to terms with his illness over the years and with the fact that one day he would pass on. My sisters took his death harder; they were younger and had been at boarding school, so they wouldn't have had as much time with him as we did. I feel so glad to have had my father for as long as I did and to have learned so much from him.

I agree wholeheartedly with Abraham Lincoln's little quote at the beginning of this chapter – 'Folks are usually about as happy as they make up their minds to be.' I think the reason I made up my mind to be a happy person was because I was lucky enough to grow up in a happy family. We weren't perfect – what family is? – but we were content. I think, in part, that contentment is down to the era in which we were born, when family life was less complicated in so many ways and there was far less stress, but I also know how hard my parents worked to provide a happy home and not to let any of their adult struggles filter into our lives. I know that not everybody is as lucky as me; some people grow up in very difficult circumstances and I always admire people who've had to struggle to get where they are because their journey has been so much harder. But we all have our struggles, and the secret is how we view them and how they shape us.

When I was thinking about happiness and counting my blessings for this book, I came across research from the very aptly named Wellbeing Programme at the London School of

Economics, which shows that the emotional wellbeing of a child is far more important than academic achievement (a good job, in my case!) for later happiness in life. I can say that that's true – my parents certainly provided me with emotional wellbeing and great confidence to overcome any early difficulties, as well as a strong work ethic and a positive outlook on life. I agree with Oprah Winfrey's view that, 'Doing the best at this moment puts you in the best place for the next moment,' and my parents always believed in doing their best, because that's all any of us can do.

I owe the person I am today to my family, to my siblings Damien, John, Susan and Kate, but in particular to my mother and father.

———

Have you called your
family to say hello or to
have a chat? One day,
they won't be there for
you to call any more.
Give them a ring and
see how they are.

2.

Overcoming
Challenges

'I have many problems in my life, but my lips don't know that. They always smile.'
Charlie Chaplin

I prefer to get on with things and not focus on challenges or periods of difficulty in my life, to keep moving forward, but I've found it very helpful to look back on occasion to see how life has taken me to my current position. Whoever said that we learn more about ourselves from our failings and challenges than our successes, I think he or she was right.

My first challenge in life, although I didn't really see it as such at the time, was undoubtedly my foot. Needless to say, I didn't go around thinking, 'My goodness, what a challenge I'm facing,' but I have no doubt that it's shaped my life in a number of ways and had its part in making me who I am today.

Times were different in the 1950s and 1960s in that 'disability', if you want to call it that, wasn't really named, as such. Maybe that's a good thing in some ways, because we weren't encouraged to label ourselves and I didn't. My foot was just part of who I was. In fact, when I was thinking about writing this book, I found it hard to recall any incident where I was conscious of my foot and its limitations. It was simply 'there'. I absolutely give my parents credit for not spoiling me in any way or making me 'special' because of it. I was just Francis, who happened to have a deformity in my foot – it didn't define me in any way or earn me any extra brownie points with my parents. Mum and Dad treated me and my brothers and sisters equally and I think that was hugely important.

To explain more about it, my foot didn't get any blood flow in the womb and my leg didn't develop fully below the knee. When I was born, my mother was told about my 'deformity' and assured that I'd never walk. She cried for three weeks, she has told me, but then she picked herself up and she and my dad set to the business of fixing it as far as they possibly could. I wore callipers to help straighten out the bones of my lower leg and foot, and my mother had a regime of nightly exercises followed by massage on my foot, which she did without fail. I had my first operation when I was just a few months old, in London, which must have been a huge effort for my parents, both personally and financially. I had had another ten major operations by the time I was eleven years old. I was in Temple Street Hospital, the Mater Hospital and then Cappagh Hospital, under Professor Paddy McCauley, who'd been referred to me by my surgeon Mr Joyce. To be honest, operations were such a part of my life that I don't have any distinct memories of that time – it's all a bit of a blur – but I do remember Christmas 1966 because I spent six months in Cappagh following one major operation. I kept a diary at the time, and it's only full of little things, but it helps me to remember the visits from my parents, who came to see me every single day – in spite of the fact that they lived in Sandyford and Cappagh, which is now in Finglas, was in the countryside at the time. I also remember a visit from Fossett's Circus, and the clown who put one of those red noses on my nose – it was like a clothes peg and it pinched. I didn't like it at all! But those hospital visits meant such a lot to me, and that's why I really admire people who make those visits nowadays. When you're sick in hospital, it can feel as though you're invisible to the outside world, so to have that connection is fantastic.

I'd be lying if I said there was no pain at all during my hospital stays and, in fact, my abiding memories of my time in hospital are connected to such pain. Once, when I was in the Mater I was strapped to the bed for some reason – I presume it was to prevent me moving my leg – and I spent hours focusing on the light hanging from the ceiling above my head to distract me from the pain.

I also remember the injections. In those days, needles for injections weren't disposable; instead, every time you used a needle, you had to sterilise it and it was then reused. The needles were stainless steel, as I remember, and they were kept in one of those kidney-shaped trays; you'd hear the rattle as the nurse came up the ward with them. Now, when I was in Cappagh, there was a strike in the needle-sharpening department of the needle manufacturers (who knew there was such a thing as a needle-sharpening department?) and so none of the needles was sharpened. I needed injections in both hips two or three times a day, and the poor nurses hated having to do it with blunt needles. I had two black hips for weeks after! Now, when I hear one of the chefs in the Park Hotel Kenmare cutting meat, that noise reminds me of the nurses pushing the needles into my hips. But I didn't complain, honestly, and I think that children don't really – they just get on with it. And besides, even at a young age, I could see how much my parents were doing for me in helping me to walk. My determination came from them. I can honestly say that I have never, ever worried about my foot, and I would always say to anybody in my position, 'Be positive'. Concentrate on what you can do in life and get on with it. I was never going to play rugby for Ireland, so I got on with other things.

I also remember a stay in Temple Street Hospital when I was about nine or ten. I'd been flying along on my bicycle, which I did in those days, and I swallowed a fly. Now, I'm sure you're thinking that that was harmless enough, but the next day I became very ill. My joints swelled up – my elbows and my knees – and my parents became very worried. So off we went to Temple Street. By now, my whole body had swelled up, and the doctors were mystified until I mentioned to my mother that I'd swallowed a fly. Then they discovered that fly larvae had somehow filtered into my bloodstream. It sounds like science fiction, I know, but it's true. At one stage, I was so ill that my mother called a priest down from Whitefriar Street, a monk with a little beard. I can still remember to this day lying in the hospital bed with this man praying over me in Latin. I thought, in my fevered state, that I'd actually gone to Heaven. I didn't understand how serious that incident was until my mother told me later that it had been touch and go. My poor parents!

As far as my foot was concerned, part of my parents' efforts involved getting the right shoes for me, which wasn't easy as there is such a difference in the size of my feet. As an adult, one of my feet is size 5 and the other is 9. Had Doc Martens been around in my time, they'd have been great! I can still remember that I used to have to go to a shoe place, Regan's, which was in a basement in Lower Mount Street, and rummage through a big pile of shoes. There was a left pile and a right pile, and I used to be only delighted to find a matching pair. However, then my parents discovered a shoemakers in Naas, George Tutty, who made specialist shoes for people like me. Today, I'm their longest-coming customer. The family have been making boots and shoes for generations and I distinctly remember that Mr Tutty used to have a room in the Royal Hotel on O'Connell Street. I'd go up to see him to have my shoes fitted – he'd make a 'last' or a model of my foot and make the shoes from that, and he still does to this day.

Thinking of Mr Tutty and the shoes reminds me of a nice 'shoe' story. I went to Kenya in 1984 with my friends from

Skål – a group of us in the hotel industry who met years ago at a hoteliers' convention and have been travelling together ever since. A party of us went on a coach trip to see the Maasai, that remarkable nomadic tribe who live in the Serengeti between Kenya and Tanzania. They wear those distinctive bright red robes and they have that interesting dance where they jump high into the air. Now, we were thrilled to be going to the Serengeti because we wanted to see the mass migration of the animals that happens there every year, and we'd arranged a visit to a Maasai village; a real place, let me tell you, not Bunratty. No photographs were allowed, and we were to be respectful at all times.

I was fascinated by the shape of the village, a compound of circular houses, and by the houses themselves, which were so cleverly built. They had a kind of corridor inside, which, instead of going straight like our traditional hall-ways, curved around to the right. And the reason for this was to put animals off because of course they can't see around corners! At the end of this curving corridor was a room, split in the middle between an eating and sleeping area. Very cleverly, the Maasai burned elephant dung to ward off mosquitoes – a great bit of recycling, even if the smell was distinctive!

Anyway, yours truly was invited to lie down on one of the beds and test out a Maasai mattress, which was pretty comfortable. The man who was showing us around, I remember, was in the process of stretching his ears – to accommodate those enormous circular earrings – with two rolls of 35mm film, which was pretty ingenious! As I lay down, he caught sight of my lovely new trainers, custom made by Mr Tutty, and pointed to them, calling others over to have a look. They gazed with wonder and appreciation at my feet and then my friend asked if he could buy them. 'Oh, you don't want to buy these,' I said, but he was very keen indeed. Could he try them on? How on earth would I tell him that one was a size 5 and the other a 9! There is no way of explaining that, so I had to hop off the bed and high-tail it out of the place!

Nowadays, my foot is part of who I am. It's always been there and I've gotten used to it, and, quite honestly, I never think about it. Now, I freely admit, as my sister Susan tells me, that I'm a great man for giving everything plenty of 'no notice'. She often says to me, 'You don't pay attention to anything,' and maybe that's true. Perhaps I just ignore things that don't warrant my attention! But I like to think that I pay attention to the things that matter, and my foot doesn't matter to me in that way because it's never held me back. I am not defined by my foot, because I'm still Francis and because I've led, and continue to lead, a very full life. There's nothing that I've wanted to do in life that my foot has prevented me from doing. I have a positive attitude, but do you know something? I've had to work on it. Certainly, I have a happy nature, but I'm a firm believer that positivity can be learned and that, with practice, our glasses can all be half full rather than half empty.

I came across this little exercise when I was researching the whole area of positivity. Write down six negative things that you think about yourself. Maybe you think you're an awful chatterbox (like myself!) or that you're too shy, or maybe you think you're always trying things but they never work out. Now, relabel those six negative things. For 'chatterbox', think 'vivacious' or 'bubbly' – people love a bubbly person. For 'shy', think 'listener', and you'll understand that your quietness can be a great advantage to you; people gravitate towards a calm person, I always think. For 'trying and failing', think 'always willing to give things a go', and you'll see that you are one of life's risk-takers – of course, you won't succeed at everything, but you'll be able to tell yourself that you've never been afraid of trying. When I think of labels for myself, I could think 'disability', but instead I think 'wonky foot', so I don't label myself as 'disabled'. Re-label yourself and see how it feels.

One thing my foot has taught me is to have more empathy for others and to be more understanding towards them. I remember once meeting a lovely boy at a book signing down the country who had a similar disability to me and who, quite honestly, was struggling with it. I said to him that life was for living and that if I could achieve everything I have achieved in life, so could he, and that the key was to try to look at his 'disability' in a new way. I think my own experiences when I was a child have helped me to have time for others, no matter what their circumstances.

As I grow older, I have to continue to be positive about my foot. I've had some back pain in the last few years, and I visited a specialist who told me that I'd probably have to take it a bit easier on the foot, because wear and tear has made it hard to stand on it for long periods of time. I know that in the years to come I won't be able to cover the miles of hotel corridor that I once did, and I'll probably have to make some changes to my lifestyle – but I'll cross that bridge when I come to it. I won't let it get me down or moan about how awful it is – I'll just make the very best of it.

I think schooling was probably more of a challenge for me than my foot because there was nothing I could do about it. Like so many boys and girls of my generation, we just endured it! However, I do remember the early days of my schooling with great fondness. We started in St Anne's NS in Milltown. My mother would send us off every day, first Damien and myself, and later Susan and Kate (John was to follow many years after). We'd be dressed identically, as was the fashion in those days. We had a lovely teacher, I remember – Miss Wright. Now, we all used to get a bun and a bottle of milk on a Friday. I was always told it was for the 'poor people', who couldn't afford a school lunch, but as far as I recall we all used to get them. The milk used to be very cold and the teacher would put the bottles in her bosom to warm them for us. I can imagine it'd be all over YouTube and Twitter now – but I was delighted with my warm milk! We loved St Anne's and the nuns looked after us very well, but after our First Holy Communion it was all change. Damien and I were sent off to school in the Christian Brothers in Westland Row, chosen because it was on the number 44 bus route. It was a tough school, I can tell you; an inner-city Dublin establishment, with plenty of boys who would take advantage if they were let. And believe me, they weren't! I remember we'd line up in the yard every morning and we'd have to put our hands on the shoulders of the fellow in front of us and not move a muscle.

Now, I can quite honestly say that the Christian Brothers murdered me. I was a normal student – nothing exceptional, but nothing awful either – but it wasn't good enough for them. For a start, everything was done through Irish and I had no notion of what was being discussed in class! It was all Diarmuid agus Gráinne, and the Táin, and Oisín and Niamh, and all that kind of thing – all very good, but I honestly couldn't understand it *as Gaeilge*! I wasn't great at Irish and unfortunately the Irish teacher was an awful man, so that didn't help. Every time he'd ask me a question, I'd get it wrong and I'd have to put my hands out for two whacks with the leather, which was like a belt with a rounded end. Once, Damien got a wallop on the leg from a leather– and you could see every stitch of the leather on his leg, like a brand.

We had to endure six years of this torture and I used to feel physically sick every morning at the thought of another day in school. I remember Karen Durham, a girl who lived across the road from us, a good Protestant, asking us once, 'What school do you go to?' when she heard us complaining about it. We answered, 'The Christian Brothers in Westland Row', whereupon she said, 'They're not very Christian, are they?' No, they weren't, and I suspect my story isn't any different from that of a lot of boys from that time. And it wasn't 'character forming' – I think my character would have been formed quite nicely without any of that kind of thing!

I've heard it said, 'We are the sum total of our experiences,' good and bad. Maybe so, but I don't think I learned anything at that school apart from how to be afraid. And, even years later, I get annoyed when I think of it. I can still remember the son of one of my old teachers, who was a particularly brutal man, coming into the Park Hotel Kenmare for a conference and asking for me. I'm not given to bad language, but I told my brother John in no uncertain terms where that man could go! I didn't want to remember my days in that place.

Now, you might say, 'Where's the positive mental attitude, Francis?', and you'd be right, I suppose. But I think the key is that, even while I recall those days with sadness, I'm not still fuming and raging about them and blaming the Christian Brothers for my woes. Like so many Irish children at the time, we weren't treated very nicely, but we got through – and I think we should be proud of that.

When Damien and I went to CUS in Leeson Street for secondary school, it was like entering Paradise. The school was run by the Marist Fathers, who had a different attitude to instilling education. They showed you everything and if you took it in, you took it in, and if you didn't, you didn't – and it didn't matter; you made the choice. This lesson has stuck with me – that so much in life is my choice, that it's down to me and I shouldn't waste my time blaming other people when it all goes wrong. The Marists gave us a good education. My best friends are the friends I made at CUS, three of whom are priests, although I don't think you can read too much into that!

The only difficulty of my time there was sport. None of us Brennans is sporty, and because of my foot I never played football or anything like that. But once, when I was about twelve or so, I got a notion that I should try something. It was spring and I learned that cricket would be starting up at the school. I thought, 'I could play that' – how hard could it be to stand around in a field and then catch a ball when it came in my direction?

Delighted with myself, off I went to Elverys sports shop and I bought the sweater and the white pants, the whole uniform. I thought I looked very smart. We headed off out to Merrion Cricket Club, which, if memory serves, was near Lansdowne Road. We weren't told anything about the rules; I was simply told to stand out in the field, and if the ball came my way to catch it and throw it to the other fielder. Sure, I didn't know the first thing about cricket! But anyway, I stood out there in the field, for what seemed like hours, in my white trousers and jumper. It was March and absolutely freezing and I thought I'd die of the cold. After an hour, a ball came in my direction at about 90 miles an hour, which

I completely missed, of course, before it bounced off a wall and into the Dodder, which ran behind the cricket ground.

Now, Father Mathews was my German teacher and he also taught cricket. He was a bit erratic, so you'd never be sure which way he'd take you. This time, he charged over, grabbed me by the collar of my white jumper and lifted me off the ground. And he roared at me, 'You're supposed to catch the f**kin' ball!'

I wasn't used to language of that kind at all and I said, 'What?'

'You're supposed to catch the f**kin' ball,' he repeated, as if I hadn't heard it clearly enough the first time.

'You're using bad language,' I pointed out to him, where-upon he said, 'I'll f**kin tell you I'll use more of it if you don't catch the f**kin ball,' and he dropped me down on the ground. Well, I was astonished at his use of language. I said, 'If this is cricket, I don't want to do it again.' And I just walked back into the clubhouse and changed into my clothes and walked home. My sporting days were over. Years later, when my parents were moving house, Mum found my cricket gear still on a hanger in my wardrobe and asked what I wanted to do with it. I said she could get rid of it at this stage!

Other than my cricket experience, I was quite a good student. I'd listen diligently and do it right, and I found that I could relax a bit now that I didn't have the threat of a beating hanging over me. I never really stood out, though, not in those days. I was quiet at that stage, believe it or not! I probably hadn't grown into myself, and because I didn't do sport I'd never be captain of the rugby team or that kind of thing. Like so many others, my schooldays were probably not the best days of my life, and I'm not sure that I would have been voted 'most likely to succeed', but I firmly believe that everyone reaches their potential sooner or later. And anyway, if you're happy, that's all that matters. When I was researching this book, I came across a quote from a Peanuts cartoon: when Charlie Brown asks Linus what he'd like to be when he grows up, he replies, 'Outrageously happy'. And I was happy – I never felt that I was missing out.

When I look back on my life, I would say that I didn't really rebel when I was a teenager. You'd probably know to look at me! But, quite honestly, it wasn't in my nature. When everybody was going partying at the ages of 16 to 19, I never partied. The height of my excitement was the night Thin Lizzy came to play in CUS! I can still remember they had a smoke machine, which had never before been seen in Ireland. I freely admit that I was conservative as a teenager; for example, I always wore a shirt and tie. In catering college, my fellow students would say, 'Here he comes, with his suit on.' I never wore jeans, like the other students, but I never really felt I stuck out either. Maybe I missed out on normal teenage things like football and parties and going mad, but it's not a sorrow. I was a bit of a nerd, before the word existed.

I also think that I didn't 'let loose', like so many of my contemporaries, because I felt a sense of responsibility to my family. I was aware that this responsibility restricted my social life hugely. I used to hear school friends talking about the 'high life' of parties at the weekend or trips to the beach, and I used to think, 'Oh, I'll be working.' But I never resented it because I never really knew any different. At the time, because Dad was so ill and money was tight, and because my siblings were still in school and Damien was in Maynooth, I felt that it was up to me to put money on the table. Family was everything to me. I've carried it with me ever since, that sense of responsibility. I always joke that if

I won the Lotto it wouldn't change me one bit because I'd still have to run the hotel and be responsible for seventy staff. But I accept those responsibilities because it comes with the territory – they grow on you so that they become second nature – and I'm happy to provide employment and a good working environment for the staff at the Park Hotel Kenmare. But responsibilities are always there and I can never fully relax or let my hair down. I have promised myself that when I retire I will be free from responsibility.

I thought a lot about responsibility for this chapter because so much of my life has been about being responsible, for myself and for others. And I think this is really important. Not all of us will be Denis O'Brien with a big company and loads of staff to look after, but we all have to be responsible for ourselves and for the choices we make in life. I think that this is essential to the whole business of happiness – understanding that we are in charge of our own lives. We don't have to blame our parents, or the Christian Brothers, or our horrible boss for what our lives are right now. We can let go of that if we understand that we are in the driving seat. Ronald Reagan said, 'My philosophy of life is that if we make up our mind what we are going to make of our lives, then work hard toward that goal, we never lose – somehow we win out.' I think he's right!

The reason I've been thinking so much about responsibility is because one of the biggest challenges I've had to face in recent years, like so many Irish people, is my financial difficulties. Now, it might seem strange to talk about this in the same context as my schooling and my foot, but somehow I feel that there's a link, because, even though I've had to work hard all my life, I've been fortunate enough not to encounter any huge obstacles; nothing that I felt I couldn't overcome with effort or thought. But this financial challenge is outside my control in so many ways – perhaps that's where I see the connection.

Now, I've written about my business issues quite openly in the press and I'm not afraid to say that I've gone through a dramatic loss in my personal wealth, like a lot of people in this country. Maybe the scale of the loss is a bit different, but it amounts to the same thing.

I write about my work in the Park Hotel Kenmare in Chapter 4, but my financial difficulties all arose from my personal pension, which I funded with profits I made at the Park Hotel Kenmare; rather than giving myself a higher salary, I'd take my profits from the hotel and look for a tax-efficient way to use them. So, along with other investors, I bought two office buildings, a car park and a share in the Four Seasons Hotel. And when the crash happened, I lost all of them, even though I'd put hard cash into them. My net value dropped by 95 per cent.

At the time, the maths seemed good for a businessman like me. You'd buy an office for a certain amount and then, when property prices rose, revalue it at 50 per cent more than you'd originally paid; with the profit, you'd refinance to put money into the next deal, and that was the way it worked. We went from deal to deal and suddenly we had a huge asset base, if no cash. And now, even though those assets have been wiped out, we're still paying rent on their full value, and it has been very difficult to sell our investments because their value is so much less. It's catch-22. I now have to pay a large amount of personal tax on a phantom rent and there's just no way around it.

But I blame nobody for this situation – and maybe that's my secret. Everybody is looking for somebody to blame, but not me. I signed those bits of paper and I decided to go into those developments, never once thinking that they would just vanish overnight. I was diverse: my money was very well spread and my investments were not all in the same sector, I thought – but there you go. Investing is not without risk, and I took the risks and paid for them. I have no pension at all now and my only option is to keep working. Now, I can understand that people might not be all that sympathetic, and that's fine. After all, on paper, €2 million still looks like a lot of money, even if it's worth little in cash. But I think it is important to remember that, Celtic Tiger or not, we still employed a lot of people. The entrepreneurs of Ireland created jobs and we're never really given credit for that.

T.S. Eliot said, 'If you aren't in over your head, how do you know how tall you are?' Well, I'm beginning to get a sense of how tall I am! I've had a nightmare for five years now and, looking back, I'm not sure how I've managed, but I have. I don't mean to make light of this; most people in my position would be looking for a bridge to jump off, but there was no bridge high enough to equal a drop in net worth of 95 per cent! Unfortunately, plenty of people weren't able to take that pressure and I can understand that, but somehow I managed to keep going. Why? Because I realised that I still had what mattered to me: my family, my work and my faith – none of that had changed. And even though my retirement plans have changed, perhaps the Lord has had a hand in things after all. Maybe He knew how much I'd hate not working and being busy, so he decided to help me out!

When I was thinking about this chapter and about overcoming challenges, I discovered other famous failures who made me feel instantly better about myself. Did you know that Bill Gates's first business was a failure? That Stephen King's first novel was rejected thirty times? That Benjamin Franklin left school at ten? These and other examples of people overcoming sometimes huge obstacles in their lives cheered me up. They also made me realise I'm not alone, my experience isn't unique, and that makes me feel so much better.

'I am not what happened to me; I am what I choose to become.' None other than Carl Jung said this, and I agree with him wholeheartedly. My early challenges with my foot and in school, and later with Dad's illness, definitely shaped me, but they didn't define me. Instead, with the support and encouragement of Mum and Dad and my brothers and sisters, my challenges gave me a positive outlook on life and a determination to keep going, no matter what. They gave me a springboard into working life and into wanting to make the best of opportunities that came my way. I was determined to work hard and to make something of my life. And, in more recent years, I've been able to ride out the storm because I've had no choice –that always helps! – but also because I can say that my mistakes are my own and no one else's. Today, I can say that I am who I've chosen to become, good and bad. I can take on life's challenges because I have my support system, but also because I know who I am, my strengths and weaknesses, and I can take responsibility for my own life.

———

Have you done something
nice for yourself today?
Treat yourself well and
then you'll know how to
treat others well. So go on,
look after yourself!

3.
Work,
Glorious Work

'Far and away the best prize that life offers is the chance to work hard at work worth doing.'

Theodore Roosevelt

About ten years ago, I met a friend of mine for coffee and told him about my plans to retire. I was forty-five; I'd been working hard in the Park Hotel Kenmare for twenty years and I felt I'd done everything I wanted to do in that area. It was time to make other plans.

My friend listened to me without saying a word, and then he shoved a piece of paper across the table to me.

'Fine,' he said. 'If you're thinking of retiring, write down three things that you'd do.'

I took the piece of paper and I wrote down three things: 1. I'd travel more; 2. I'd do Lourdes more (as you may know, I accompany groups on trips to Lourdes); and 3. I'd do more media. Ten years on, I'm doing all three things on my list and I'm no nearer to retiring! Now, as you know from the last chapter, some of that is down to necessity and I certainly haven't had as much choice in the matter as I'd like. But I understand that perhaps a life of leisure isn't for me. In fact, I'd say I'm busier than ever and I'm loving it. To me, the key to happiness is a life filled with things that interest me.

I know that some people work to live, but I'm the opposite. I love work! It gives me a sense of purpose and helps me to focus my energies on the things I really love doing. I agree with Steve Jobs when he said, 'The only way to do good work is to love what you do.' And I do love what I do and feel that I've been so lucky in that respect. From childhood, I had an innate work ethic that's just propelled me through life. I've also been fortunate to do work in which I've had a fair amount of control over things, which, experts tell me, is essential to enjoying work. Even in the early days as a deputy hotel manager, I was able to run things as I wanted, within reason, and then, with the Park Hotel Kenmare, it was 'my show', with the responsibilities that came with it, but also the freedom to follow my vision for the hotel. I'm also a big 'team' person and it makes me truly happy to work with other people both on *At Your Service* and in the hotel – it comes naturally to me. That's why my job matters so much to me, because it allows me to express all the things that I'm good at.

However, if you'd told me when I began my 'proper' working life in 1973 that I'd be busier than ever at sixty-two years of age, I'd have laughed at you. When I left school, having gotten my Leaving Cert, but with just one honour, my top priority was to get a job that paid reasonably well, because my parents had retired at that stage and yet they still had three children in school. So I began as a salesman in a 'piped' TV company called Marlin Communal Aerials, when piped TV was in its infancy. Piped television replaced the aerials that everyone used to have on their houses; instead, the signal came through a series of cables that ran from house to house. At the time, it was all completely unregulated and basically you could run your wires everywhere; there were wires all over the country!

My boss must have recognised my gift for chat, because my job was to go to the difficult customers and talk them into having the wire to connect them to the TV. The way it worked was that if one person said, 'No, I don't want that wire,' no one else around them could have the TV, at least not without great difficulty. Of course, each housing estate would have six or seven 'difficult' customers, and I had to sort them out.

I quickly developed a strategy to get around them. I'd call to the door and I'd say something like, 'If you don't take the wire, poor Mr Brown in number 24, in his wheelchair, who is totally housebound and is relying on TV as his only source of entertainment, well, that poor man will never get television.' And once I'd laid the guilt on, I'd add, 'And I'll give you twelve months' free TV, if you let me put the wiring in. You won't see a thing. I'll put it over your wisteria, under your rose beds, around your ivy...' I knew every plant in the country! I'd be miles ahead with talk and persuasion, full of that ironclad self-belief we all have as youngsters.

On the other hand, the man who trained me, a man called Mr Henderson, wasn't cut out for the job at all. He was terrified of all customers; to steady his nerves, he'd have to drink at least two pints of Guinness in order to knock on a door. And the customer would run him anyway because he was so bad at negotiation. He'd be having endless pints of Guinness to no avail!

I discovered at Marlin that I was a born salesman. I never had a refusal, ever, and everyone was happy with the service. Since I'd have every customer covered by the Tuesday afternoon of my working week, I got a second job at the Step Inn in Stepaside, where I worked as a barman and loved every minute of it, earning great tips. Sadly, the TV business wasn't going quite as well, in spite of my efforts with the customers, basically because the company would tell the customers fibs about when they'd be getting their TV – there are seven people in Clonskeagh who still don't have it to this day. I have to admit, I still keep my head down when I pass those houses in Clonskeagh.

I didn't like their business in Marlin, so after a while I said to Mum that I was thinking of going back to catering college in Cathal Brugha Street. You might remember that I'd taken some time off to run the shop and earn a few bob. Well, I only had one Leaving Cert honour and I needed two to do the diploma course in hotel and catering management, so I went to see the principal of the catering college at the time, Bob Lawlor, and told him about my night work. He said, 'I'll tell you what, we'll make an exemption and you can do the course, even if you only have one honour.' Which is proof that the interview is the important thing. I'm a believer in the interview, because I think you can persuade people of your worth much better that way.

However, having persuaded Bob, I then decided I'd aim high and do a degree course, rather than a diploma. This would add an extra year onto my studies. It also meant that I'd need to redo my Leaving Cert, to get the extra honour – I was never a man to make it easy for myself! But, do you know, all of a sudden I was a good student, because I was doing subjects I liked: Economics, Business Organisation, Accountancy, Home Economics and French. I sat those five subjects for the repeat Leaving Cert and got four honours in the business subjects. I'm a firm believer in doing things that you are passionate about, and my passion was business and hotels. I suppose I also did well because I was actually applying the practical side of those subjects in my work life. In fact, I can still remember taking the number 44 bus to my Business Organisation exam and opening the textbook for the very first time on the bus, because I already knew so much from work and college about invoicing and payments and banking. I think there are certain areas in life in which there is really no substitute for practical experience.

In total, I spent four and a half years in Cathal Brugha Street, learning the business that I'd wanted to be a part of ever since I was a child. I continued to work hard and stay busy because I still needed the money, but I also had a lot of fun doing so. I think when you're young you have tons of energy and will try anything at all! But happiness is about keeping that enthusiasm for learning and trying out new things all the way through life. You're never at the point when you know everything; there's always something new to learn. I think that doing new things is important, not just because it keeps you fresh, but because it can really boost your self-confidence. I would never have thought that I could achieve four honours in my Leaving Cert after my early ex- periences in school, but doing just that really made me feel good about myself. And it was the same with work – the more I learned about my trade, the more confident I became.

When I was at college, I was in charge of student em- ployment – a valuable way for the students to get experience and for the hotels to get staff. In those days, it was actually quite hard to get people to work – a lot of young people came from farming backgrounds and there was loads of money in farming at the time, so staff were thin on the ground. However, I did my best!

Organising staff was a bit of a task, not just because of the shortages, but also because of the quality, which was uneven to say the least. I used to hire this fellow called Fingers – so-called because he was absolutely hopeless and dropped everything, but beggars can't be choosers. One night, we were doing a dinner for the Masons at King's Hospital School in Lucan. Of all people to be working that night, it was Fingers. There were various toasts, to the school and that kind of thing, and of course lots of Masonic goings on, and then, lo and behold, there was a toast to the Queen. And in the brief silence before people lifted their glasses, who should yell, 'Up the Ra!' at the top of his voice? Only Fingers. I'll never forget it. There was silence in the place, I can tell you.

Another spot I remember was the Pelletier Hotel on Harcourt Street because we used to do a lot of functions there, and, frankly, I learned a lot about triumphing over adversity there! The kitchen was in the basement, but the function room was four floors up, on the top floor, so we'd have to bring everything – food, cutlery, plates – past reception, tripping over the Japanese tourists checking in, and up the stairs. It was the worst B&B in Ireland – worse than Fawlty Towers! However, they did have lovely crockery, which they'd gotten from the legendary Jammet's Restaurant when it closed. But they never had enough of it, and what they did have weighed a ton. One night, we had a function on and we ran out of soup bowls. One of the waiters began to panic, but I thought on my feet. 'Listen, table one, are they finished?' When I found that they were, I took the bowls, gave them the quickest wipe with a serviette and resent them out to table ten! One of the waiters was scandalised, but it certainly beat trotting down four flights of stairs to wash bowls and trotting back up again, by which stage table ten would have been starving – and they were only delighted with their soup! I can assure you that I have higher standards nowadays at the Park Hotel Kenmare.

I was learning a lot about the job and loving every minute of it. I really thrived on the constant variety and being able to think on my feet. And even some of the more 'interesting' hotels were good to work in – and when you're young, you don't bother about that kind of thing; you just get on with it and concentrate on having fun. But I'm not sure I'd be able for the Pelletier nowadays.

I still needed to earn a few bob, though, and there was no money for a youngster in the hotel business at the time, so, like many Irish people of my generation, I set off to get factory work during the summer. I can still remember this summer so well because it was that hot one of 1976. I'd gotten a job in a canning factory, Smedley's, which was near Wisbech in East Anglia. A friend of mine had been there the year before and had said that the money was great if you were prepared to work hard. And I always worked hard! As it happened, it was a terrific learning experience in the food processing area, which helped me in my chosen profession.

Summer in Smedley's was all about peas. Peas are in season only for a few weeks of the year, and every day a procession of Roadstone-sized lorries would arrive in the factory, full of peas to be processed by the Irish boys and Maltese girls in the factory. Yours truly was in charge of the hoppers, big containers into which the lorries reversed their loads. Now, at this time, Wisbech was very dangerous, and they didn't like the Irish, so we never really ventured out. I got a little business going buying in Mars bars from the lorry drivers for 20p each, which I'd sell on for a profit; I did this with newspapers too. I made a few bob! And it passed the time because the day was long in Smedley's – 7.00 a.m. to 10.00 p.m. The Irish were quite happy, of course, because, really, we were only there to make money.

My job was to keep an eye on the hoppers as they started revolving and to feed the peas into a 2-foot conveyer belt, which would hop along and carry them into little troughs and then onto a giant conveyer belt into the factory. I also had to rake out all the peas that didn't make it into the factory and put them into a container for animal feed. You should have seen me, running from one hopper to the next and by the time I'd get to number five having to run back to number one, because otherwise it'd get clogged up and the caterpillar would stop going around and you'd have to put that line off. Now, if you've worked in a factory you'll know that it was the end of the world to put a line off. The workers were paid .000000001p per can, which might sound tiny, but remember we were processing millions a day. However, fewer cans meant the workers inside were losing money – and they'd eat you alive in the canteen. Conscientious old me here never let a line go down.

I was outdoors during the hottest summer in years and was brown as a berry, but, being me, I wanted a bit of variety so I said to my supervisor, Bob, 'Go on, give me a turn inside.' So he put me on the conveyer belt where the peas would be checked before being dyed. Yes, every processed pea in the world is dyed because they lose that lovely green colour in the cooking process, but it's a natural dye. The peas are then cooked in the tin. The peas came along a channel four feet wide for a visual inspection by people on either side of the conveyer belt – it was pretty monotonous work. I'd hear from the Irish fellows that they all got the knack of falling asleep at the conveyer belt whilst moving their hands to make it appear as if they were looking for defective peas! After a while, I'd get off the seat and lose my balance because my mind would still be focused on the peas. I begged to be put back outside on the hoppers.

'I'll put you into the freezer; it's much better,' Bob said. At the time, excess peas that couldn't be canned immediately were put into the blast freezer. I was given a big parka jacket and off I went into the freezer to bash the peas to unstick them so they wouldn't block up the whole system. Can you just see me?! I did this for half an hour on and half an hour off for two or three days, and then Bob put me on the line where peas came off the freezer. Here, I'd have to get huge plastic bags ready for the load of frozen peas, which involved arranging the bag on a kind of Meccano structure on a fork-lift, putting a corner of the bag on each bit of Meccano; the frozen peas would then be tipped into the bags. It could be perilous work, because a ton of frozen peas is pretty dangerous. You could be killed by frozen peas – imagine! We had to work really fast, making up one bag as the other was being filled and so on. Some bags would be too battered to use, and you'd be fiddling around trying to open another one, while someone was yelling that the peas were coming. Everything was against the clock – rush, rush, rush. If you stopped, peas would fall on the floor and you'd be eaten by the supervisors. Factory work is not for the faint-hearted and I absolutely salute anyone who does that kind of work, because it's really tough.

Thankfully, canning peas was not to be my life's work, but I learned a lot about being quick, flexible and trying to have a bit of fun, no matter what I was doing. I think there are some jobs you can really only do when you're young, and working at Smedley's was one of them!

My next jobs were to teach me more about the hotel business, good and bad, and gave me a great grounding for my working life. First, I worked on Jersey in a hotel called the Cheval Roc, run by an ex-engineer from the Royal Navy, Wace Philo. He was a lovely man and the most organised in the world. There was a day for every job: on Tuesdays you oiled the hinges on the windows; on Wednesdays you watered the carpet in the bar – yes, watered, because they had a pigskin carpet. I also learned the essential art of turning taps off fully and then giving a little quarter turn back, because that way your taps will last a lifetime. A little tip from Francis!

I have particularly fond memories of Wace Philo because I learned such a lot from him. Mr Philo was a patient teacher, I have to say, and never raised his voice to me, even when I flooded the hotel, as I did once. Water supply is a problem in Jersey and the hotel had its own well, which was way up on a hill above the hotel, so water pressure was pretty poor. One day, for some reason, I had to go up to turn off the water supply to the hotel, and I turned both taps off. Needless to say, I wasn't supposed to and Mr Philo asked me to turn the red one back on. However, he didn't tell me that when I turned the taps back on water would come thundering back down the hill and through the system, bursting the pipes in the attic. We had a massive flood, but Mr Philo didn't give out to me; he simply suggested that in future I turn the tap on very slowly, so that water would trickle through the system. I became an expert on water pressure!

I'll never forget how kind Mr Philo was to me, a youngster who really didn't have a clue, and how much I learned from him. He was such a man for detail and precision and would never settle for something that was half done. I took those lessons to heart and have kept them with me. Mind you, I didn't always impress. I remember that I used to mix Brandy Alexanders, which were all the rage back then – a mixture of brandy, ginger and cream, which had to be shaken in a cocktail shaker. Needless to say, I once shook too vigorously and ended up spraying myself with Brandy Alexander. Mr Philo thought it was hilarious. It went all over my shirt and I only had two shirts, so I had to change it and come back down to the bar. But I couldn't have been that bad because when I left the hotel, Mr Philo said, 'Do you know, Francis, I've never had an assistant [manager] like you. You were the best.' I think you really only need a bit of encouragement and patience when you're learning the ropes and I try to give this to the younger members of staff in the Park Hotel Kenmare. Otherwise, sure, how would you learn?

I suppose I learned the most as a young hotelier from my stint as a trainee deputy manager at the South County Hotel, as it was then, in Stillorgan, Co. Dublin. They say that you learn more from adversity than from ease, and that was certainly the case in the South County. My experience there was really a prime example of how to make something out of nothing, and I learned to think on my feet, an essential part of the hotel business, as well as DIY, animal extermination and a whole lot of other skills!

The South County had been owned by everyone and anyone at that stage – P.V. Doyle, the Rank Film Group and then two brothers who had a butcher's business in Lamb's Cross. The brothers didn't have much patience for the hotel business, it has to be said. One night, they got fed up with the hotel and decided to put everybody out there and then, locking the front door behind them. The hotel sat there for another ten years, exactly as it had been left. And I mean exactly! The tables were all set and food was still on plates! As you can imagine, it became alive with mice because of the food, and the ceilings, which had been lowered to keep the heat down, and covered with those lovely polystyrene tiles, were now home to 200 wild cats. Then, when the hotel was taken over by two businessmen, Mike Ryan and Mike Murphy (not to be confused with the broadcaster of the same name), a gang of people were called in to tidy the place up.

The two Mikes were new to the hotel business. They leased the hotel for £600 per month and hired a Mr

McGough from Australia to run the hotel. He had a formula for this kind of thing and it had always worked for him. First, he opened a nightclub, Sardi's – a huge bar and dancefloor which could fit 3,000 people – which was the talk of the place at the time. Everybody wanted to come, even though it was £8 to get in, which was a lot in the 1970s. It was considered to be the height of glamour, with cocktails served with umbrellas, which was fairly exotic for the pint drinkers.

The brothers' instructions to Mr Gough and to the staff had been to whitewash everything, but our basic problems had never gone away, if you catch my drift. The place was still full of wildlife, and concealing the fact took some energy, I can tell you. I can still remember that there was banquette seating along one wall, in a big, sweeping curve, and the mice used to run along it. I'd approach customers to ask if they were enjoying their dinner, stamping my feet on the floor to scare the mice away. They'd still outwit us, though. One night we had six girls in for a hen party. They were very jolly after their drinks when one of them said to me, 'Excuse me – I think there's a mouse on the dessert trolley.'

I feigned ignorance. 'Oh, no – a what?'

'There's a mouse on the cheeseboard,' she insisted, 'and he's eating a Ritz cracker.'

I had to think fast. 'You see all those bushes outside,' I said to the girls. 'Well, they clipped them earlier today and disturbed a field mouse.'

I got away with it that time, but other times I wasn't so lucky. I remember the dance floor had those revolving coloured lights – they were all the rage at that time – and one night a mouse went onto the dance floor, and every time he went to go off it a light would move and he would be mesmerised – he started doing circles on the dance floor. He was terrified, the poor little thing. We had to shoo him off.

Whatever about the mice, the cats were worse because they were lingering in the roof, since no one had thought to get rid of them. One night I was in the restaurant; the music was going and I was dancing along to *Saturday Night Fever* when I heard a scream: one of the ceiling tiles had fallen down on the floor in front of an elderly couple.

I went over and said, 'Terribly sorry. Did the tile hit you? Sometimes when you open the front door there's a bit of a breeze.'

'No,' the elderly woman shook her head, looking mystified. 'There was a cat – it fell out of the roof.'

I feigned astonishment at the very idea and she turned to her husband and said, 'Now, Tommy, I shouldn't have had that second glass of wine.'

I said, 'Don't worry, we'll get you plenty of black coffee and you'll be fine.'

Another night, one of our feline friends was going mad, making an awful racket meowing and scratching around in the ceiling. One of the customers was looking up curiously and pointing.

'I'm sure I can hear something up there,' she said. 'It sounds like a cat.' And she looked as if she couldn't believe it herself. As usual, I had to improvise.

'Oh, yes,' I said. 'We have a long-stay guest, Mrs Murphy-Moose, and she writes poetry. Have you ever heard of her?'

'No,' said the lady, looking interested. 'Maybe I'll get her out of the library.'

'Oh, yes,' I agreed. 'I'd recommend her. But, you see, she has a cat here, even though she's not supposed to, and it must have slipped out of the room.'

This poor lady is probably still looking for Mrs Murphy-Moose in the library!

Working in a busy hotel like that, survival is often a matter of attitude. I know that my sister Susan, who worked there too, absolutely hated the place. She'd have to have two baths after every shift! However, I thrived on the adrenaline and even though the place was ramshackle, to say the least, I enjoyed every minute of it and learned such a lot.

One day, my ingenuity was really put to the test. Just before his daughter's wedding in Foxrock, a proud dad was sitting on the arm of the sofa in the lounge, pint in hand. His daughter was sitting on the sofa beside him in her finery, waiting for the wedding car. Then a cat fell out of the ceiling, hitting Dad on the arm and knocking his pint all over his daughter's dress. I was on duty at the time and so I ushered the bride upstairs to take off the dress. Then I bolted off in my mustard Mini to the IMCO dry cleaners in Stillorgan, dress in hand, to see what could be done. I ran in the door and explained my predicament, whereupon the man behind the counter took hold of the dress, put his foot on a button and poured cleaning fluid on the stain. After a few minutes the dress was spotless, so off I went again in my mustard Mini, back to the hotel. The dress was a bit damp and the bride was forty-five minutes late for her wedding, but her dress was saved and I got away with it.

Getting away with it was the order of the day in that hotel, and even though quality left something to be desired I learned all about keeping the customers happy. Sunday lunch was a case in point. The hotel served what they grandly called 'Indonesian Rijsttafel'. I know, did you ever! Only gorgeous, darling! In case you don't know, rijsttafel means 'rice table' in Dutch and it's supposed to be a kind of tapas or mezze-style meal, with a range of little dishes. The good people of Ireland weren't exactly familiar with the name, but at £1.59 for this buffet lunch the place was alive every Sunday, even if there was never enough food for the hungry hordes. Initially, we only had twenty customers, but by the time we got it going 170–200 people were turning up for lunch. So miracles had to be performed to serve them! I'd come in on a Sunday morning and the restaurant tables would have been left from the night before, and then the chef would ring in sick and we'd have to make the few bits and pieces of food stretch to cover 180 people. I'd be boiling potatoes and all sorts; the thing was to serve the cheapest food possible, so there was an awful lot of liver and bacon in our rijsttafel! I suspect the Indonesians don't go in for that kind of thing, but in Ireland in the 1970s people weren't all that fussy. In fact, when Susan appeared with a new bowl of something to put out on the glass shelves (which made the buffet look about twice the size), she'd have to cut a swathe through the customers, who were attacking her with their knives and forks because they were all starving!

'They have no manners, those people,' she'd say indignantly when she came back into the kitchen.

All we ever provided for dessert was jelly. I do remember, though, that we were one of the first places to get one of those centrifugal cream machines. You put in a pint of cream and mixed it with water and the machine made fluffy and economical cream. Needless to say, the machine was half broken, and you'd have to plug it in and then run back and forth to keep an eye on it.

One night, I remember, Susan pulled a little too hard on the door of the fridge and the whole thing slipped forward and twenty bowls of different coloured jelly came flying out.

And, of course, we just scooped it up off the floor and served mixed jelly in bowls, which we called tropical jelly. The next week, everyone wanted that mixed jelly. I like to think we've come a very long way in Ireland in terms of our eating habits!

I also learned the not-so-subtle art of spotting theft at the South County. I worked Friday, Saturday and Sunday nights in the bars, of which there were five at the hotel. Brennan here would collect cash from all the tills at the end of the night to balance it up; it was a matter of pride for me to be able to reconcile it to the last penny. But of course it never balanced; there was always money missing. I remember this one night we had about 2,600 people in and there was no way the takings reflected that – we were missing a cool £1,000. I suspected one particular barmaid, and when I quizzed her on the missing money, she explained, 'Well, you see, Mr Brennan' – she held up her hands to show me her talons – 'those buttons aren't made for my nails. I'll press something and another number will come out, or two receipts.' She finished innocently, 'The nails are causing the problem.' As stories go, it was one of the more novel, but there was such a volume of business that things like this were often overlooked in the hotel.

I can tell you now that I never helped myself to a penny. I'd finish up work in the early hours of a Monday morning, have a shower and head off on the 46a bus to lectures, with just my wages in my pocket.

The South County had been something of a baptism of fire, but the hotel business is so much about being a bit ingenious and solving problems that it really stood me in good stead.

When I started in the hotel business, the customer was always right no matter what, and I learned that in

Parknasilla, where I cut my teeth as a young duty manager, first on a 'stage' or internship in the summer of 1978 and then later when I worked there. At the time, Parknasilla was part of the Great Southern Hotel Group. Now, the hotel was always overbooked, for some reason, so there was always trouble; there was also no elevator at the time, which some of the guests didn't like. I got into the habit of meeting the tour buses and climbing on board to say, 'Hello and welcome! If anyone has any ailments, would you please tell me because there's a lot of stairs.' Some guests weren't able to go up the stairs without getting a dose of angina between the front door and their room!

I remember one lady in particular who didn't like her room because it was small and poky, and she came down to complain to me.

'I'm not staying in that room,' she announced, and then she improvised, 'because I have a heart condition.' I could tell that she was only delighted with herself for having thought of it so quickly.

'Well, Madam,' I said. 'I did ask you to tell me if you had any health conditions, and I'm afraid that's the only room available.' Whereupon she began to cry, and the next thing what looked like two spiders fell onto her cheeks. I nearly died. What's happened to her, I thought, trying to keep a straight face. Without a word, she just picked her false eyelashes off her face and put them back in her purse – and off she went to room eleven, because that was the only one that was available.

I also remember that Queen Juliana came from Holland to Ireland on her holidays when I was in Parknasilla. She wasn't staying at the hotel – no room eleven for her!; instead, she was staying at Reen-na-Furrira, Nuala Roche's (of Roche's Stores) home in Sneem, Co. Kerry, the Roches having been asked by Bord Fáilte if they'd lend her their home. The deal was that the Roches could stay in Parknasilla any time they liked as compensation. Now, at the time, the son of the family – we won't mention his name – was a demanding teenager. I remember some mornings hanging onto the pillow for the last bit of sleep, when word would come up to me that Mr Roche wanted a red apple and they only had green ones in the kitchen – that kind of thing – and he only thirteen.

One day, I was in the back office working away and I heard a commotion at reception. 'Excuse me?' I knew by the voice that it was Mr Roche and that he was talking to Stella, our receptionist, who was a lovely girl and the fastest typist in the West, but not the brightest. Oh, God, I thought, how is this going to go?

'Could you tell me what time high tide is?' Mr Roche enquired.

Without hesitation, I heard her reply, 'Oh, it's at 11.02.' How on earth did she know that? I wondered. Maybe she was in the yacht club or something. Not wanting to stifle genius, I didn't say a word there and then, but I couldn't go home without finding out. So, later on that day, I said, 'Stella, tell me, how you knew what time high tide was?'

'What do you mean, Mr Brennan?' Stella looked mystified.

'Well, it's a complicated enough thing,' I said. 'Did you learn about it before?'

'Oh no,' she said. 'I worked in Mulranny [the hotel in Co. Mayo]. It's on the sea.' And she looked at me as if I was the biggest eejit!

'I see,' I said politely. 'And tell me, Stella, did you do a course?'

'What do you mean, did I do a course?'

'In tides, I mean.'

'Of course I didn't. High tide was at 11.02 every night in Mulranny.'

I had visions of Mr Roche perched on a rock with the waves coming over him, and thinking, 'I'm sure she said 11.02 ...'

Now, it was the 1970s and the IRA was all over the place at the time, so the Roche house was ideal for Queen Juliana because it was on 300 acres and very secluded. My job was to go up to Queen Juliana from the hotel and take her food order for the evening, which consisted of uncooked ingredients because she liked to cook herself; then I would come back later with the order in a box. As you can imagine, security was intense around the estate and there were gardaí everywhere. Then, on the fifth or sixth night of her stay, the IRA raided Parknasilla late at night. I wasn't on duty, but they got hold of the poor unfortunate other junior manager, stuck a gun in his ear and got him to open the safe. There was never much money, maybe £300, but that wasn't the point. Having gotten the money, the boys drove up the avenue of the hotel and threw the money out the window – it wasn't the money they came for; they were giving the two fingers to Irish security services. Funnily enough it ever made the papers, but everyone knew about it.

At the time, my boss was a man called Brendan Maher. Now, he was an excellent manager and I learned a huge amount from him, not least the importance of excellent customer service, but he could be a tyrant and he used to reduce the staff to tears quite regularly. I don't think he was really aware of the impact he had on people. One Christmas morning, I distinctly remember he bawled out some poor girl over something and she burst into tears. I went into him and said, 'What are you making staff cry for on Christmas Day?' He didn't say a word, but he simply went home and didn't come back for the rest of the day. I don't think he really had a clue what he was like until then. It was an early lesson for me in keeping everyone happy and in understanding that your behaviour can affect other people, and I've tried to remember that ever since. The hotel business is a pressurised one and we can sometimes lose the run of ourselves, but it's important to set an example. In fact, when I was reading about happiness for this book, I read an article in the *Washington Post*, which said that working for a 'bad boss' can contribute to poor mental as well as physical health, in particular high blood pressure and even heart attacks! So, if you're guilty as a boss of micromanaging your staff, criticising instead of encouraging or being negative when you don't need to be, maybe it's time to look at your management style. At the Park Hotel Kenmare, we try to encourage our staff and lead by example, rather than telling them what to do.

Of course, times were very different in the Ireland of the 1970s and 1980s. I was effectively doing the job of food and beverage manager in Parknasilla, but, as was often the way in Ireland at the time, I wasn't getting paid for it. I was basically being paid a trainee's wages, and I knew that with my experience I could have been doing better. So I went to see Colm Rice, the boss of the Great Southern Hotel Group, who quoted me some report to say that I hadn't got the relevant experience. I can remember that my old friend Breege O'Donoghue thought I was mad to be making a fuss. She had started out with the Great Southern Hotel Group, and is now executive director of Primark and a superb businesswoman. 'Listen here,' she said. 'You are getting a marvellous education. You couldn't possibly leave over money. Don't be always worrying about the money; there's much more to life than money.' But that wasn't the point for me at all. I felt that I should be paid a salary that reflected the job I was actually doing and the responsibilities that went with it. The Great Southern Hotel Group always lost the best talent over money and had no policy for bringing able and talented people up the ladder, so they lost all the youngsters who were good. I learned the lesson early on about bringing people up the ladder, and I always apply it at the Park Hotel Kenmare. If you're great in the bar, we bring you into the restaurant, and if you're great at reception, we make you duty manager. We bring people with us. I firmly believe that is the only way to do things.

By this stage, I had a lot of good experience under my belt and I was only dying to move up the ladder. The idea of owning my own place hadn't yet taken shape in my mind, but I was definitely ambitious, and then, as is often the way in life, I got an offer just when I most needed a boost. A Dutch businessman, who had just bought the old Great Southern Hotel in Kenmare, asked me to come and see him. Now, for reasons I won't go into in too much detail, the locals were wary of this man because he wasn't 'one of us', but I decided to take the risk. It was Christmas and as I left Parknasilla, I joked, 'If I'm not back at five, send out a search party.'

Once I arrived at his beautiful house, he offered me afternoon tea, which I accepted, and we both sat there, chatting for a bit. And then he got to the point of the meeting: he wanted to offer me the job of general manager of the Great Southern in Kenmare, which he had great plans for. I know I was ambitious, but the idea of getting that old hotel up and running again was too much for me. Ambition has to be tempered with realism every now and again!

'Oh, I couldn't possibly do that job,' I said.

He insisted, 'Oh, I know by the way you work in Parknasilla. I can see that you have talent and would be up to the job.'

And do you know what? I said no! The money would have been great, but I felt that I had still too much to learn. As I said earlier, sometimes it pays to know your limitations, and, at this stage, I just wasn't ready for a big job like that. But I knew that I was ready to move on, and when I saw that there was a new hotel opening in Cork called the Victoria I went for an interview there and they offered me the job of deputy manager. I left Parknasilla in February 1979 and off I went to work in Cork. Working in a new hotel was a great experience because we had to buy everything from mattresses to toothpicks. The Victoria was really Ireland's first boutique hotel. Also, it was revolutionary at the time because there was no ground-floor space. Robin Power, the owner and property developer, had bought the building and installed retail units on the ground floor, getting huge rents on the shops as well as rent on the hotel above. It had never been done before – genius!

After a year, the general manager retired, and I went for an interview for the job. Now I felt I really was ready, having learned a lot at the Victoria, and I asked the board to decide whether or not to give me the job in February 1980. And then, lo and behold, my Dutch businessman friend from Kenmare appeared out of the blue at the hotel one day and asked to see me in the bar. He put all his plans for the re-vamped Park Hotel Kenmare (formerly the Great Southern) out on the table and talked me through them. 'I asked you before and I'm asking you again,' he said, adding by way of explanation, 'My last general manager took off in his BMW because he couldn't take Ireland anymore.' It turned out that the poor general manager, being from Holland, couldn't get his head around Ireland at all! Suppliers would say they'd come on a Tuesday but they wouldn't come until Thursday – that kind of thing.

I had a lot to think about, but I still wasn't persuaded – and then I got a little help from the board of the Victoria. The board told me that, even though the general manager had retired, they were going to leave me as deputy manager for another six months to earn my stripes because I was too young. Well, that decided me. I left on a Friday and off I went to Kerry to take up the job at the Park Hotel Kenmare, which reopened in July 1980.

I was just twenty-six, which was fairly young, but what I lacked in years I made up for in enthusiasm and drive. Mind you, I got my first lesson in spending my money wisely fairly early on. Pope John Paul II had visited Ireland in 1979, as you may remember, and we hired the tent he'd used to say mass to throw a huge party for the great and good to celebrate the opening of the hotel. As I remember, the tent took a week to put up and a week to take down. In the week running up to the party, it rained torrentially; water ran off the roof of the tent and seeped in under the carpet, which we had installed for the party. We ended up hiring these huge machines to suck the water out of the carpet. It was still wet on the night of the party, which was all right until the ladies, in their Rocha and Givenchy, decided to sit on the carpet – every time one of them got up there was a plate-sized damp spot on her dress!

No expense was spared by my boss. He chartered a plane that went from his native Amsterdam to Paris and then on to Cork Airport, from where a bus took the guests to Kenmare. He hired an Irish piper to play the pipes on the last leg of the journey. The poor man had to wait all day in Cork Airport because the flight was delayed, and then he greeted the guests beautifully on the red carpet. All this was fine, but once the piper arrived at the hotel with the guests the boss wanted him to play in the lounge, which he did until he fainted halfway through, falling on the bag that supplied the pipes with air – there was an awful noise. It turned out that he hadn't had any breakfast! Piper apart, the party was a big success in terms of PR coverage, but it cost a fortune and did nothing for the hotel – not a single booking or conference came from that party. It was a good lesson, and I'd try not to make the same mistake myself – wasting money on things that don't get bookings. But, tent or no tent, I was well and truly on my way.

Now, I haven't analysed my working life; I've just gotten on with it, and I've enjoyed every minute because I've had the great good fortune to be able to do a job I love. We had some fantastic years at the Park Hotel Kenmare and some difficult ones, about which more in the next chapter, but I have had to sit down and think a bit about why the job has made me so happy. After all, this is a book about happiness!

I remember when I was at school all the talk about the future was that it would be the 'age of leisure', when machines would make our lives so easy we'd have all the time in the world to sit back and relax. Instead, technology has had the opposite effect – it has made life busier and more complex. And because lots of us work 'flexibly' and we bring our work with us everywhere, this can mean that basically we're working all the time. Is it any wonder that the workplace can be very stressful for some people and that work-related illness is increasingly common? At the same time, work satisfaction is going to be more important than ever in the future, even from a government's point of view – because economies won't be growing so much, we'll all have to think of other ways to measure our happiness, aside from the size of our wage packet. I'm not sure if this emphasis on work satisfaction is to distract some of us from the fact that our wage packets haven't grown much in recent years, if at all, but I do know that happiness does not equal money. The other thing is that, like me, many people won't be retiring on the dot of age sixty-five, so finding work we enjoy is all the more important. They say if you find a job you love, you'll never work a day in your life. I've definitely found that to be the case. So I think we all need to think about 'work' and what it means to us; it's all very well for me to work all God's hours because I love my job, but I know that many people don't, and in our 'always on' culture I think at least we need to reflect.

I love my job because it's always 'new', no matter how long I do it. There's always a new customer with a new request or dilemma; there's always something new to be done to the hotel because we're in a business where you constantly have to look forward; and even though the problems can be somewhat similar, there's always somebody new to meet on *At Your Service*. So I never really have the sense that I'm doing the same thing over and over – no *Groundhog*

Day for Francis! And John and I work hard to make the hotel a happy place to work for the staff. I read a very interesting article by a man called Professor Cary L. Cooper, who is a work and happiness expert. He quoted a managing director on the magic formula for happy staff. In this managing director's company, Communisis, they 'Give their staff "wriggle room", don't micro-manage, let people know when they have done a good job, make them feel part of a family and ensure reasonable work–life balance.' That sounds to me like a formula for happy workers.

—

Do *something* every day
that you love; whether it's
fishing, cooking, reading
or walking the dog –
you deserve it.

4.

Park Life

My biggest challenge in my working life was certainly the opening of the Park Hotel Kenmare in 1980, when I was general manager. Remember my meeting with my Dutch friend in the bar of the Victoria in Cork? Well, that was to set me on a very exciting and challenging path – a path that I'm still on today. I'd never have thought, when I was clearing mice off the dance floor at the South County or counting peas at Smedley's, that one day I'd own my own hotel. It was certainly something I'd dreamed about, ever since putting on Dad's taily coat, and I knew by that stage that I had a head for business, but I'd never really put it up there as a 'goal'. And yet, here I am!

Now, when I started as general manager in the Park Hotel Kenmare in 1980, the Irish hotel business was a much older person's business; that's probably why the Victoria had been so reluctant to promote me to the position of general manager. At the Park Hotel Kenmare, we were only kids. I was twenty-six. My head waiter, Andy, was a young fellow, too. Sure, we were willing to do anything at all to look after our guests. As general manager, I also didn't mind getting my hands dirty: I'd carry the bags and say hello to the guests and do any little jobs around the place. I never thought that such and such was a job for a chambermaid and that kind of thing. I just got on with it. I remember once a guest saying he had a puncture. I said, 'Give me the keys and I'll fix the puncture, and tomorrow your car will be ready' – now, I didn't get the jack out myself, but I made sure it was done!

I have been known to go to great lengths to ensure customer satisfaction and one of my favourite memories involves looking for a goose. Now, this is a long story, so settle down!

It was 1981, when the hotel was still open year-round, and we'd had an enquiry from a Canadian company based in Cork. Their new factory had just been completed and the company had decided to treat all its employees to a 'thank you' weekend. No expense was to be spared, even though the contract to build the factory had overrun by millions of pounds and there was uproar about the whole affair in the media and in government. Those were the days!

I had planned a holiday for the latter part of January and the group was due the first week of February. Two days before I was about to leave, I got a call from Canada to say that one of the VIPs had requested an 'Irish goose' for the gala dinner and to ask if I could arrange it as a surprise. Of course I could, I replied confidently. I would be holidaying in Mum's home place and I knew plenty of people around there with geese.

When I got to Sligo, I mentioned it to Mum. She was a bit negative about it because most geese die for Christmas and they'd be few and far between at the end of January. However, always optimistic, I set off to meet Peter, a fowl merchant who lived locally and who I'd known for years. Like Mum, he said that there wasn't a goose to be found west of the Shannon at this time of year. Uh-oh, I thought. Got to get a goose!

I decided to leave Sligo a day early and head to Kerry via Dublin, where Pat Walsh, my father's fowl merchant, still traded, to secure my goose. Surely he of all people would have one. But after a detour of 250 miles, no goose could be found. I was in a panic at this stage, but I hadn't yet run out of ideas – I still had my old friend Mrs Cronin in Carrigaline, Co. Cork, who had supplied me with geese when I ran the Victoria in Cork. So, 200 more miles later, I arrived in Carrigaline to warm greetings. But, no, Mrs Cronin did not have a goose.

'Oh, wait,' she said. 'I might have one frozen in the walk-in deep freeze. Will I see?'

'Yes please,' I said, following her into the deep freeze. It reminded me of my days in Smedley's in Wisbech all those years before. We trawled through every chicken, turkey, Cornish hen, pheasant, snipe and goodness knows what else – but no goose.

It was now Monday and the party was due to arrive on Friday. I still had one ace to play: in Kilgarvan, near Kenmare, I'd often spied geese along the banks of the Roughty River where it flowed through a field at the back of a local B&B – I would try there.

Now, on leaving Sligo I had commandeered my brother Damien's VW Scirocco sports car. To this day I can still feel how wonderful it was to drive and it really did look the business. I left Cork gooseless and drove back to Kenmare in the Scirocco. On the Tuesday morning I drove down the long road to the B&B. On my arrival, two big dogs appeared and took an instant dislike to the car. Needless to say, I was terrified to get out and called out, 'Hello!' from the safety of the car. There was no reply, so I honked the horn. Eventually the door of the house opened slowly and the lady of the house appeared. I introduced myself and apologised for not getting out of the car, because I was afraid of the wild dogs. 'Sure, they're only pets,' she protested as they showed me their teeth.

From the safety of my Scirocco, I launched into the story of my search for a goose. I told her I really hoped I could rely on her as I'd often seen her geese in the field beside the house.

She shook her head. 'I've never had any geese.'

I assured her that she had – I had seen them beside the house.

'Oh, they're seagulls,' she explained. 'They often come up this way from Kenmare Bay.'

I couldn't believe that I wasn't able to tell the difference between a goose and a seagull after all these years in Kerry. Maybe I needed my eyes tested, I thought. I was completely speechless, which is rare enough for me!

The lady directed me to Dan Joe, the manager of Kilgarvan Post Office, who would know everything via the postmen of the area. Red-faced, I thanked her and headed for the post office in my Scirocco. In I went to one of those little shops that has absolutely everything in it, from stamps to spades, and I introduced myself. After a bit of banter, I launched into my request. Dan Joe said he didn't know anything about where I might find geese himself, but he'd just run next door to ask the postman, if I could wait.

I sat myself down on a stack of 2lb bags of sugar to wait, and next thing a car pulled up outside and I heard great shouting and greetings. This must be the postman, I thought to myself, marvelling at how the Kerry people were so willing to help and what a great man Dan Joe was altogether. After about twenty minutes of chat outside, with great enthusiasm and back-slapping, I thought I must be getting somewhere, but then there followed another ten minutes of chat, after which Dan Joe came back in to the shop.

I jumped up all excited. 'Well?' But no, the man in the car was the captain of the Kerry football team and he'd just stopped to say hello and pass on greetings to Dan Joe from his wife. In the excitement, Dan Joe had completely forgotten about me. It was all I could do not to scream! But things move slowly in Kerry.

Dan Joe shot out of the door and into the postman's house, and came back with the great news that there were geese to be found out the Bantry Road. I jumped off the sugar bags, ecstatic.

'There's just one problem.'

'What?'

'The woman's a bit … reclusive. She's a bit psychotic and you'll have to tread carefully.'

'What might she do?'

'Well, she often waves a shotgun at people to frighten them off.'

My God, I thought, I might end up with more pellets in me than the goose. But still, if I wanted my prize I'd have to brave it.

I headed off, thanking Dan for the help, and was just about to sit into my car when Dan roared after me. 'Have you tried Clifford's?'

Clifford's was, at that time, the bakery in Kenmare. Now, I bought all my bread for the hotel from Clifford's, even though it was a little more expensive. The gentle Mr Clifford was the only man in Kenmare who came through my door seeking my business and we had struck up a great friendship. What would a bakery be doing with geese? I wondered.

'I'll put a call through for you if you go into the phone box,' Dan Joe said, nodding towards the phone box. Dan cranked up the exchange and put me through to the bakery. As I waited to be connected, I felt sure that I had found my goose and that Mr Clifford had saved me from the gun-toting eccentric on the Bantry Road. At least she could be my back-up!

One of Mr Clifford's sons answered and I ran through my story. He told me that his brother looked after that side of things and he'd get him for me. My heart lifted, and when the other son came on the line I ran through my spiel again. My heart sank as I heard his hesitation. Well, they did have geese, he said, but not at this time of year. Oh, God, I thought. It was Thursday and I had to get that goose by Friday.

And then he said that they did have one goose …

'I'll pay anything for it,' I said. 'And I only want one anyway.'

'Well, it's actually a bit of a family pet,' he explained.

Who on earth has a goose as a pet? I wondered, whereupon he explained to me that it was eight years old and had escaped the table thus far.

Now, if you are of a culinary disposition you'll know that eight years is pushing it as far as a goose being edible goes; they are usually at their best before their second birthday. But I prevailed upon him and hinted that giving me a goose this size would do wonders for the sliced pan business at the weekend, whereupon he capitulated. The poor goose was brought up to the hotel on the Thursday night and by Friday was served to our guests, who loved it.

But the story doesn't end here. Twenty years later, I was interviewing for the position of commis chef at the hotel and I had about eight applicants, one of whom was the daughter of the lady at the B&B who'd assured me all those years before that I was only seeing seagulls. Great, I thought to myself. I'll get to the bottom of it when she comes in for interview.

We went through the usual formalities and then I got to the matter of my visit to the B&B. I didn't mention any seagulls just yet. Did her mother still do the geese at Christmas? I asked.

'Oh, yes,' she replied. 'Mum and Granny sell about twenty or thirty geese every Christmas and it's great seed money for the few treats, you know.'

I couldn't resist it then. I had to tell her the story of my visit all those years ago. 'I couldn't believe that your mother had no geese and nor could I believe that my sight was so bad that I couldn't tell the difference between a seagull and a goose!'

The girl broke into laughter and told me that, to this day, her mother still worried that the man in a suit and tie pretending to be from the Park Hotel Kenmare might turn up again, when she knew full well that he was really from the Revenue, checking up on the poor farmers and their wives who were only trying to make a few bob!

Our VIP lady who'd requested the goose was a very satisfied customer. Given the difficulty I had in sourcing it, I probably could have served an old boot covered in gravy and tried to pass it off as a goose. But I believe in going the extra mile for my customers and trying my very best to make them happy. I'd never have dreamed of trying to pass off some other bird as a goose, because it would have stayed with me that I'd short-changed the customer. My policy of service came from my dad and from working in his shop, and I'm proud to say that we were way ahead like that.

Thanks to Nuala Roche, who did a fantastic job with the interiors, we had a lovely hotel – absolutely glorious at the time. We were lucky because when we opened there weren't enough hotel rooms for American guests in Ireland, so we benefited from that. I do remember one guest saying to me that the Park Hotel Kenmare was, 'What every American imagines every European hotel should be'. This was because it had very good service, very good food and lovely facilities, and yet it was an old Irish house. What we created was perfect, to be honest – a lovely family atmosphere but with the best of everything, including the best service and the best crystal, which I'd hunted down from everywhere. We were offering something different at the time, and for me it was the realisation of a dream.

There was only one slight drawback. The owner at the time wanted to open all year round, which in a seasonal business was a nightmare. We had 55-plus staff for three guests in March! During the winter of 1982–3 I fought with the owner to close, but he dug his heels in because he was a self-made man who didn't like to show local people that he didn't know what he was doing. It was a matter of pride, I suppose. But pride was losing us a ton of money.

Unfortunately, it was only a matter of time before he got into trouble. I prevailed upon him to close the following winter, and off I went on my annual sales trip to the US. Word came out to me that cheques were bouncing all over the place, and when I came back from the US at the end of March 1984, a liquidator had been appointed to the hotel. We only owed £11,000, which wasn't a lot, really, but times were different then and companies were pretty tough about getting their money.

The owner took a turn and ended up in hospital, leaving me in full control during the crisis. When I met the liquidator, I found out that the owner had structured the company very unusually, in that the building was owned by a Swiss company and the management by a company in Ireland – so the management company had no assets, just its trading. I had to tell the liquidator that this terribly complicated arrangement was nothing to do with me. I hadn't been involved in it. Now, I was meant to be a director, but – the Lord is wonderful – I never signed the papers, simply because I was in the US at the time. So when it went belly up, I was just an employee and not liable for the hotel's debts. And then I had a brainwave: I asked if I could lease the hotel from the liquidator and open in April of that year.

I said to him, 'Isn't it much better for you to have the hotel up and running and making money rather than closed and dead, and we have a very busy summer coming up and word will get out that the hotel is in liquidation.'

The liquidator wasn't a bit sure. 'Oh,' he said, 'that would be most unusual. I'd have to check with the judge.' And so off he went, and the next thing I found myself opening the hotel at Easter. It was the beginning of a nerve-wracking and exciting few years.

By then, the seed had been planted in my mind that maybe I could buy the hotel outright. The only problem was that I hadn't a penny! So I asked my mum and dad for the deeds of their house and I borrowed £40,000 on the house. I know, there aren't too many parents who would agree to this, but my parents never said a word because they trusted me. However, getting that loan was another matter. I won't mention any names here, but I visited one bank, let's just say in the area, along with my good friend Nuala Roche, to see about a loan. I went into the office and the official was sitting behind a huge desk with nothing except a phone on it – it looked very Big Brother! I said that I'd like to open an account please and he replied, 'I want nothing to f**king do with the Park Hotel in Kenmare.' I suspect he hadn't been on good terms with the owner.

Now, Nuala Roche was a proper lady, and you didn't use bad language with her. 'Do you know who I am?' she enquired.

Bold as brass, he said, 'I do.'

She told him in no uncertain terms that she'd move her business elsewhere, whereupon he replied, 'In relation to the Park Hotel in Kenmare, I couldn't give a f**k.' Well, Nuala was like a lion! We marched out, opened an account at another bank and reopened the hotel on 7 April 1984. I was on my way.

I'd promised the liquidator that if he sold the hotel within six months of me leasing it, I would just walk away and I wouldn't look for anything; my company would cease to exist. So I was taking a big risk, and I was aware that it was with my parents' money. But I knew that it wasn't a problem. I felt confident that the Park Hotel Kenmare would thrive.

You might remember that in those days credit cards were really only beginning to take off, so when you accommodated credit cards as a business, you had to apply for a machine and then a permit to use it, which would take a couple of weeks. This was fine, but there was a catch: when I used the machine to process transactions, I wouldn't get any money from these transactions until three weeks later. So, from 7 April until about mid-May, I wouldn't see a penny. But I needed money because I was capital light. And one or two of our creditors, who shall be nameless, didn't help – they wanted their bills paid. Two fellows in trench coats, like they were in the Mafia, arrived in search of the cash, and they wouldn't give me their services until I paid up, plus an extra bond in case I went bust in the next ten months. Now, I say this not to settle scores but to show just how difficult it was to start a business in Ireland at the time. Credit was near to impossible to get and a myriad of other obstacles were placed in the way of entrepreneurs; thankfully, it's a different matter nowadays.

There was one benefit to my credit card dilemma, however. Because I couldn't take cards initially, I told everyone, 'I've just started a new company and I'm running the hotel myself, so you'll have to give me a cheque or cash... but you can post it on to me afterwards.' Everybody was delighted – I didn't have one bad debt and I had cash flow up the wazoo. Things were so good, in fact, that I kept the credit card story going until the end of May to keep the money flowing in! On 19 April, I went to the bank and I paid the £40,000 loan back and returned the deeds of the house to my parents. There was no question in my mind that I wouldn't repay them, but it felt good to do it so quickly.

At the time, the dollar was nearly 1:1 to the pound, so it was a bonanza for our American guests. We were full from the day we opened to the day we closed after that summer. However, the money men (and they were generally men in those days) were looking at twelve-month figures, so in this context they didn't look very good. In fact, it appeared that we were losing £600–£800,000 a year. But I understand how hotels work; you have to cut your costs in October to March, when you don't have guests, so you're not paying wages to 55-plus staff to do nothing. I know that this might sound unfair to some, but the hotel business is a seasonal one and that's the only way to do it. In Kenmare today, it still is. The town is alive between Easter and Hallowe'en, and much quieter in the winter.

Anyway, the upshot of this was that companies interested in the hotel would come in to talk to me and then they'd look at the books and go away again, because the hotel didn't look like a viable business. So the minute the hotel closed that year, the liquidator took over the reins. He couldn't sell the hotel that first year; in the second year, he looked at me and I looked at him, and he sighed and said, 'I have no option, do I?' And I said, 'No, you don't!' So off we went again. I opened again in 1985.

Now, during this year it all got very interesting in the hotel business. Ashford Castle was bought by a syndicate, which included Tony O'Reilly, Chuck Feeney and others, for a huge sum of money. The syndicate was set up to avail of a loophole in the US tax system on buying old buildings with antiques. Then Dromoland Castle was sold in the same way, and before too long a delegation came to the Park Hotel Kenmare to talk to me. It would be a perfect match for the syndicate – a top-level hotel on the west coast. I was quite excited because, as you can imagine, it would have promoted us into the same league as Ashford or Dromoland. We were already a five-star property, but an affiliation with Ashford or Dromoland was a geographical plus. Most American tourists travelled to the west coast and would now have lovely hotels in Mayo, Kerry and Clare to stay in.

The syndicate representative said to me, 'Draw up a plan for what you want to do with this building. Decide, say, that you want to spend £3 million to be spread out over the forty-seven rooms and we'll put the price on that for the syndicate to buy it and make a profit.' I suggested various improvements, which he included in his plan, and off he went to the liquidator to discuss the price. I wasn't privy to this, of course, but I was to be given a five-year service contract to run and to develop this top-class new Park Hotel Kenmare, with a proper function room for weddings, because we didn't have one, along with a swimming pool and improvements to the rooms. As you may know, the hotel business just eats money, because you constantly have to upgrade and refurbish, so for me this was a golden opportunity to do what I wanted with the hotel.

It seemed that we were all set. But then, at the beginning of 1986, somebody in the US noticed that people were making a lot of money buying up old hotels with antiques and Ronald Reagan promptly closed the loophole in the tax system. Here we were, all set, and at the eleventh hour the deal was gone. The liquidator was nearly out of his mind!

However, my circumstances had changed. Thanks to the lack of a credit card machine, I now had a substantial sum of money in cash. I won't reveal how much, but it was a lot for a relative youngster. My accountant Pat Sheahan said to me, 'With that money and your track record, you could probably borrow the rest to buy the Park Hotel Kenmare.' The thought had never even entered my head. I mean that: never. I was actually looking at a place near Limerick, something with fourteen bedrooms that I could turn into a lovely country house hotel and not have to borrow a penny into the bargain! And I had a pretty convenient situation in the Park Hotel Kenmare because, remember, the moment I closed the hotel I was gone and the liquidator was back in charge.

But Pat was enthusiastic about my buying the Park Hotel Kenmare. 'You can leverage the money you have,' he insisted, and so we did up our plan and off we went to visit the banks in Cork. I'd be in one door in a brown coat and out another in a black coat, in one door in a blazer and out another door in a suit. Over two weeks, I went up and down that South Mall to thirteen banks, with a very good business plan and every penny of my money in it – and they all said no. It's too big a deal, they said, and you're too young and the risk is too much. So no Irish bank would back me.

'Can you think of anyone else?' Pat said, and then I remembered this one guest we used to have, a lovely man from Geneva who was in banking and who'd always said, 'If you ever want to do anything, let me know, Francis, because I'd love to talk to you.' Pat egged me on to ring this Swiss banker about the Park Hotel Kenmare. I did so, and he said, 'Send me your business plan and I'll look at it and come back to you.' He rang me up a couple of weeks later – there was no email or fax in those days – and he said, 'Come over, because I have a proposal.' Off I went to Switzerland to find that he was prepared to lend me the money. The liquidator sold the Park Hotel Kenmare to me in 1986, a full six years after I'd begun to work at the hotel.

Owning my own hotel was something I'd only dreamed of, so to find it a reality in my early thirties came as a bit of a shock, even though I myself had put together the deal. I think we can surprise ourselves sometimes by what we're capable of doing, and I try to remember that when I'm having a go at something new. 'Francis,' I say, 'you might surprise yourself.' And I often do! That's why I'd always say to people, 'Feel the fear and do it anyway.' Don't let lack of self-confidence hold you back or prevent you from doing something you really believe in and want to do. I sometimes wonder what might have been had I not thought I could do it, or had Pat not encouraged me – maybe I'd still be a general manager, and that'd be fine, but I'm glad I took the risk.

It was completely unheard of for an Irish person to borrow money from abroad at the time. There was a risk of course, because the Swiss franc could fluctuate against the pound, so I was always very anxious about my loan being in Swiss francs. The way the loan was structured was that furniture, fixtures and fittings were secured on a fixed yearly fee of £25,000, which I had to repay every month over ten years, and then there was a separate loan for the building at the commercial rate. This will be important later!

It was all set and I was the owner of the Park Hotel Kenmare – but nobody knew! I didn't want to tell Mum and Dad or anyone else, because on the outside everything was the same and I didn't want to worry them. I just kept going. I really wanted to make the hotel a success. Of course, when you become a success everyone wants your business, and soon enough a Dublin bank came calling and sent a representative to see me. Little did he know, I was dying to refinance because of my worries about the Swiss franc, but when he said that he wanted 17 per cent interest – interest rates went up at one stage to 40 per cent at this time – I ran him out of the place. I was outraged, as you can imagine. 'Why would I change to 17 per cent when I am repaying at 4 per cent?' I said. 'Do you know what?' I told him, 'You can pay for your own lunch and go home.' There's a tough side to Francis Brennan, you know! Three weeks later, he phoned with a much better deal, and so it was time to get out of Switzerland.

I have to say, the Swiss were astonished. When I went to see my Swiss banker friend and told him that I was going to redeem, he said, 'Nobody ever does that.'

'Well,' I said, 'I'm going to, because I want the loan in punts. Now, what discount are you going to give me on the furniture?' Remember, every year I had been repaying £25,000 of my furniture loan plus a big pile of interest. By my reckoning, there was £600,000 outstanding, so, between the jigs and the reels, I had about £240,000 to play with to refurbish the hotel. With this money, I did a huge job – I doubled the size of thirty-one out of the forty-seven rooms. I now had a hotel that was almost twice the size it had been before – and I owed exactly the same amount of money. A brilliant financial stroke, even if I say so myself. Maybe this reveals a tougher side to me, but I've always felt that it's just business and I try to be level-headed about it. You have to take emotion out of business. And, as it turned out, I was very lucky I'd managed to refurbish, because the year after I'd upgraded the Sheen Falls hotel opened. With such competition close by, I'd have been written off, I know that. The hotel business is a competitive one, I can tell you.

We did the building job during our closed period of 1989–90, between Hallowe'en and Easter. It was controlled chaos, as I liked to call it. An arch was built to link the old part of the hotel with the thirty-one new rooms. What I'd planned to do was build the blockwork up to a certain level, then leave it while we opened for Christmas so we wouldn't have a great big wall obscuring the views, and then start again in January. However, while I was at the Red Sea on holidays, I got a phone call from John Moriarty, the barman, to tell me that the builder was progressing so well he wanted to keep going with the blockwork; in fact, he already had, and all you could see out of the existing bedroom windows was a 30-foot wall! I was delighted about the building work being so far ahead of target, but I was terrified about how the guests would react to their 'Christmas view' of an abyss of darkness!

On 8 December, I was flying to London on business when I spotted an ad in *Cara* magazine for battery-operated LED Christmas tree lights, and I had a eureka moment. When I got to Heathrow, I rang the number given in *Cara* and ordered forty sets. I returned from London triumphant with a suitcase full of Christmas lights. Outside each existing bedroom window we placed a barrel with a Christmas tree in it, attached our lovely LED lights and put the control box on the window sill inside so the guest would be in full control of the display. Tony Hanahoe, the footballer, used to come every Christmas with his mum and dad, and when I asked his mother if the building work was bothering her, she said, 'Where do you have any building? I can't see out the window because I have a gorgeous Christmas tree and I can turn it on and off, and I feel like a child in fairyland.' My scheme had worked perfectly.

When we reopened that Easter, I had the loan back in Ireland and everything was as it should have been. We were set for a lovely fifteen years with no troubles and no worrying about the Swiss franc. My mother often gives out to me that I never asked for help. 'We never helped you,' she says. But I was happy to do it all on my own and I didn't want to burden her with any of it. I'm like that – I always just want to get on with it. I have to admit it's a weakness of mine, not to look for help, and I wouldn't recommend it!

I don't mind saying that the refurbishment saved the Park Hotel Kenmare, because the hotel business eats money. Every year you have to do something: wallpapering, carpets, beds. It never stops, ever; it's a continuous cycle of spending to keep everything up to date. And that's fine when business is good, but when it's down, as it has been for all of us over the past few years, you have no money to spend and that becomes a problem. But all that was to come.

The Park Hotel Kenmare was a great place to be in the 1990s and we all had fun making the whole thing work. The staff and I worked well together as a team and, as is often the way when you have a tight-knit team of people, we were able to have a laugh every now and again.

I remember the lovely Mary Cunningham, one of the waitresses, with great fondness. When we opened the hotel in 1980, we had a great à la carte menu – it was of a very high standard, I remember. You wouldn't see such a menu now because, in these days of casual dining, customers wouldn't know what it was about, but back then it was very 'proper', as I like to call it. Now, Mary was a gorgeous girl, but she was always in trouble. I had beautiful uniforms made out of lawn fabric, which I'd gotten from Liberty in London, and Mary would dry hers on a bush rather than on the line that our housekeeper Mary Kermath had helpfully provided. Mary K had worked in Claridge's and was a brilliant housekeeper, and she was horrified that Mary C would just throw Mr Brennan's lovely uniform on a bush to dry! When Mary K came barrelling into the restaurant looking for her, Mary C hid behind the curtains!

Now, we used to serve this beautiful consommé with a pastry topping and it was called a consommé Charles II, because it must have been given to King Charles at one stage. We used to present all the food on a big silver tray, so off the waiter would go to the table with each course on the tray, and he or she would present the dish by name: 'Madam/Sir, your consommé Charles II'. Then he or she would put the tray on a side table and serve the soup. Of course, poor Mary would often be scattered and she'd forget the name of the dish. This one evening, as she left the kitchen with her consommé on the tray, I could hear her whispering to the other waitress, 'What is it?' because she couldn't remember.

I don't normally do this, but this particular day I was sitting with guests in the restaurant. Out she came, down to the table, and announced loudly, 'Here's your soup.'

I explained to my guests that we were just doing a bit of training and I said gently to Mary, 'No, Mary, that's not quite right.'

She looked confused for a moment and then brightened. 'Oh, I know,' she said. 'Your consommé.' And she put the soup down on the table.

'No, Mary,' I insisted quietly. 'You'll need to go again.'

She thought for a few moments, then a lightbulb went off over her head. 'Oh, yes, consommé Henry VIII.' Right soup, wrong monarch, but I didn't have the heart to correct her!

I was also very fond of Liz Gaine, our receptionist, who could type at the speed of light but didn't always check what she was typing. Now, there's always tension between reception and the kitchen over the menu, because it has to be typed by the receptionist and yet the kitchen doesn't really decide on the menu until the very last minute. So poor Liz would type the menu and run off twenty-five copies and then the chef would decide that he wasn't doing jelly, he was doing jam instead, and he'd want to change it; or he'd return from his afternoon break to find that girolle mushrooms weren't available and he had to replace them with button, and so the menu would have to be redone. Needless to say, Liz became very adept at waiting until the last possible moment to do her typing, generally at 6.55 p.m. for 7.00 p.m. service, much to the panic of the restaurant. I'd hear it every evening: 'No, they're not done yet...,' and then the sound of rapid typing at 6.55 p.m.

One day, as usual, someone from the restaurant came in looking for the menus and poor Liz became very agitated. 'I'm not done yet,' she said. 'Look.' She threw the handwritten menus at the waitress. 'The chef will ring me in five minutes and tell me that the drizzles didn't arrive.' Liz never knew what she was typing; she thought that the 'drizzles' that she saw on the menu – 'a drizzle of olive oil,' etc. – came in a box from the greengrocer.

Another key member of staff at the Park Hotel Kenmare was John Moriarty, the barman, who is still with us at the hotel to this day. Now, hotel people are great for practical jokes, as it helps to be able to have a laugh behind the scenes in such a formal environment, and on this one particular occasion John Moriarty was the victim. It was the year of the Millennium, and we'd been terribly busy for Christmas and the New Year, so I decided to take the staff off to Las Vegas for our annual holiday. A few days before we were due to leave, a hard shell suitcase appeared in the front hall and remained there.

Eventually I asked, 'Who owns the suitcase?' fearing that a guest might have left it behind.

'Oh,' one of the girls told me. 'That's John Moriarty's.'

Now, our lovely housekeeper at the time, Joanne, decided to play a practical joke on John Moriarty and she roped in my brother John, who knew the combination to the suitcase as he'd borrowed it once before. I came upon the two of them taking all of John M's clothes out of the suitcase and replacing them with magazines from the lounge. There were also two grapefruit sitting on the reception desk, left behind by a guest, and I have no idea why but I threw them into the suitcase as ballast. We were thoroughly enjoying ourselves, wondering what he'd make of it when he got to Las Vegas and opened his suitcase to find a ton of magazines and two grapefruit in it. (And, in case you're wondering, we did put John's clothes and toiletries into another bag to bring with us – we weren't that mean!)

Off we went on our holidays, overnighting in Shannon. I felt sure he'd open the suitcase in the hotel in Shannon, but, no, he had an overnight bag for that purpose. So the following morning, as we made our way to the airport, John still hadn't discovered what was in his suitcase.

We got to the check-in desk and John was first in line with his overnight bag and his enormous suitcase. He was asked the usual security questions:

'Did you pack your bag yourself.'

'Yes.'

'Did anyone give you anything?'

'No'. Little did he know! And then, for some reason, John misheard the woman at check-in and thought she'd asked him to open the suitcase.

I thought, Uh-oh, if he opens the bag, he's going to say, 'What's this?' at the top of his voice and the whole airport will be alive with security. We'll all be locked up for the day.

I marched over to him. 'What are you doing, John?'

'The lady asked me to open my bag,' he explained, proceeding to put the combination into the lock.

'She did not,' I said smartly, as the surprised ground hostess looked on.

'She did,' he insisted, and before I could do anything the case was open and a grapefruit hopped out. I gave it a good kick to get it out of the way, pushed the suitcase closed again and, ignoring the rogue grapefruit, ushered him up to security. John was by now fuming at having been man-handled and I had no choice but to explain the practical joke. He found out that Joanne was involved and he ate her alive. He was raging and he didn't see the funny side of it at all. And then Joanne got into a sulk and promptly said she wasn't going!

'Listen, Joanne,' I said firmly, 'you are going to America, because your suitcase is on the plane. Have you any idea what it's like to get a suitcase off an American plane? If you want to come home straight away, that's your choice, but you are going.'

So we all went for our breakfast in stony silence. I spent the whole flight panicking that a sniffer dog would set upon the suitcase when we got to the US! I can't say I blamed poor John Moriarty for his reaction, because we really did get carried away that time.

Richard, another of the barmen, was a lad of whom we were all very fond at the hotel. He was from Sweden and, even though he was only sixteen years of age, he'd written a nice

CV and sent it off to the Park Hotel Kenmare. I remember he'd been raised by his mum and granny, and he was a lovely boy. Now, he had a hearing problem, which sometimes led to misunderstandings. One night, for example, some American guests went for a walk in the garden and when they came back they said, 'My God, we were eaten alive by midges at the bottom of the garden.' Richard was puzzled because he couldn't understand why a lot of little people were lurking down at the bottom of the garden!

Richard had beautiful, stylish clothes – unlike the Irish – but he'd run out of clean everything and didn't know the first thing about washing clothes, because his mother had done everything for him, so we told him there was a launderette down in the village and off he went to use it. He was confronted by a machine that he didn't know how to use, but he had great help from the owner who told him the cycle would take forty minutes. Oh, Richard thought, I'll just go and ring my mother. So off he went. And when he came back to the machine, he noticed it was open.

'Thanks very much for taking my clothes out of the machine,' he said to the owner.

'I didn't,' the owner replied.

Someone had come in and stolen his gorgeous Swedish clothes. We were watching for weeks afterwards to see if anyone in Kenmare looked unusually stylish! The staff had a whip-round for him to replace his clothes – not that you could buy that kind of style in Ireland at the time, but I think he appreciated the thought. I donated a six-pack of socks!

And then there was Seamus, another lovely boy who worked with us. I'd always do the flowers, maybe putting a bit of sweet pea in the rooms. This particular day, I said to Seamus, 'Just get me six sweet pea, Seamus. I don't want anything else.' And I sent him off down to the greenhouse at the bottom of the garden, where we had a wall of sweet pea. I was at reception checking people in and out when I saw Seamus walking down the corridor with six 6-foot whole sweet pea plants, which he'd ripped out of the ground. Our sweet pea plants for the year were slightly diminished. Seamus says he'll never forget the look I gave him – he learned his horticultural lesson.

It was a marvellous time to be in the hotel business; as well as the fun we had in the staff room, we had lots of entertaining guests. I remember one year Keith Richards and Ronnie Wood from the Rolling Stones came to stay. All was well at first: they had dinner in the restaurant and then retired to their rooms to strum their guitars. At about midnight, a call came down to reception from one of the guests, complaining about the 'racket' next door. I had gone home at this stage, so Ken Connolly, my assistant, went up and knocked at the door of Keith Richards' room and asked them nicely to quieten down. Half an hour later, there was another complaint and up Ken went again. This time, he went into the room, which was in a haze of smoke, to find Keith Richards lying on the floor on his back, with no clothes on, playing away on his guitar.

Ken, eyes averted, said, 'I'm sorry to ask, and I know you need to practise, but we've had a few complaints and can you just keep it quiet?'

'Who's complaining,' naked Keith Richards asked.

'Well,' Ken said nervously. 'It's another guest.'

'Well, I want to make a complaint about the complainer,' Richards retorted, a bit put out.

Ken said, 'Well, that's fine, but the complainer still isn't happy, so can you turn it down a bit?'

Sure enough, the lads turned the volume down, and the next day they came down to reception and paid the bills of the guests who'd been in the surrounding rooms. 'In case the complainer was in one of those rooms,' Keith Richards explained, which was very decent of him.

We also had John Travolta on a few occasions, which set the staff aflutter. This wasn't very long after *Saturday Night Fever* and *Grease* and he was a superstar. One Christmas, I remember, he rang down to ask for laundry service. Mary Healy, a lovely quiet girl from West Cork, was dispatched to his room to fetch his laundry. She knocked on the door, was handed a bag and was about to walk away when he said, 'Hang on a minute,' and he began to unbutton his shirt before handing it to her to add to the bag. Poor Mary was mortified. I don't think she understood how lucky she was!

We had lots of other guests, including Burt Bacharach, Hal David and Kathy Bates, none of whom got up to anything, I'm pleased to say. They were all lovely guests. I do remember that Michael Nyman, the composer, came to stay once. At the time, he had just written the soundtrack to *The Piano*, so he was really something. Now, by coincidence, a tour group called Backroads Bicycles was on a break in Kenmare and they came over to the hotel to ask if they could watch *The Piano*, which they'd gotten on video in the town, in our cinema. This was fine by us, so off they went to put it on, unaware that the composer was staying in the hotel.

My mother was also staying at the hotel for a few days and as she came out of the restaurant with her friend Rosaleen, John Moriarty piped up, 'Mrs Brennan, *The Piano* has just started on the big screen if you want to watch it.'

Oh, great, thought my mother, I've heard all about that film. So off she went, assuming, for some reason, that John was also coming. The cinema was in complete darkness by the time she arrived and the film was just beginning. Now, the opening scenes of the film are a bit raunchy, and my mother, mistaking the person beside her for John Moriarty, who she knew well, gave him the elbow. 'Did you see that, John?' she whispered. 'My God.' And then the screen lit up and my mother discovered a very embarrassed young man from Backroads Bicycles sitting beside her. The film got even raunchier and my poor mother thought she'd faint, but she felt she couldn't get up and step over the man sitting beside her after elbowing him, so she had to sit through the whole thing. Meanwhile, Michael Nyman was sitting in the lounge sipping tea, oblivious!

In the mid-1990s, my brother John joined me working at the Park Hotel Kenmare, helping initially with the marketing and promotion of the hotel. John had followed me into the hotel business, and by this stage he'd been working for the Sligo Park Hotel as sales and marketing manager, having worked his way up through the industry. Then, quite suddenly, a deal fell through and he found himself at a loose end. He was only married to Gwen a year at that stage, so I said, 'Why don't you come and work with me? There's tons of space.'

'Oh, I'm not sure if Gwen would like to live in Kerry,' John said, but they came down anyway for a look around, and one night we went out for dinner. Unfortunately, I chose a local Italian restaurant, the manager of which was a bit temperamental, and on the night in question, when I was eager to impress John and Gwen, there was a full-blown row. A few girls came in and asked for lasagne, and the manager replied that he didn't have it. They told him smartly that he didn't have it the time before either, or the time before that.

'Well, I put it on when I want to – everything is not always available on the menu,' he barked, whereupon there was a ferocious row and he threw them out. I thought, Oh no, poor Gwen will think Kenmare is awful – and this was even before the girls came back and went at the manager again! But I must have done something right because John and Gwen sold their house and moved to Kerry. And then along came baby Adam and then baby Ruth, and Kenmare became their home.

John brought a fresh approach to the hotel and lots of new ideas. I had been quite happily tootling along, but, rightly, John said, 'We need to look to the future. A lot of our guests are elderly and we're losing business because they are passing on. We need to get the demographic down.' Now, at the time, spas were just beginning to be the new thing in the hotel business and I'd met some people to talk about building one at the Park Hotel Kenmare. I'd even gone to Switzerland to look at the Biotonus spa in Montreux because they were looking to open a branch in Ireland at the time. However, I was slightly put off by the 'medical' nature of the whole thing – the Swiss take their spas very seriously! Their biggest seller was the unborn sheep placenta, which they'd inject into your spleen to extend your life – I nearly died when I heard this. I'd have had the protestors outside the hotel with placards about the poor sheep! I think that lamb placenta would just be too much for Irish people.

I had put the project to one side, but John revitalised it. 'If we're going to build a spa, it needs to be a proper one, not a swimming pool where people jump in and out,' he insisted, so off he went all over the place to spas like Chiva-Som in Thailand to see what they were about. Then, at my friend Martin Skan's hotel, Chewton Glen, I bumped into a lovely lady called Susan Harmsworth. Susan had a marvellous beauty and spa business called Espa and I suggested that John talk to her – and so our next project at the Park Hotel Kenmare was born.

Now, spas are designed to be full of light upstairs, and then you descend through a tunnel into the gloom – it's supposed to mimic coming from the womb into the light and vice versa. And we have a lovely spa, even if I say so myself! It's called Sámas and it's very popular. Many years later, everybody had a spa, but we had to register and grade it accordingly, and today the Park Hotel Kenmare is one of only two destination spas in Ireland – the other being Monart. I have to say, spas are marvellous, but I'm not a spa person myself. I've been to one or two, in the interests of research, and I nearly suffocated when they wrapped me in tinfoil and put sage and thyme on me; I thought I'd die of the heat – I felt like boil-in-the-bag food!

Our spa has been a great success, but, even more than that, we've achieved John's goal to bring down the average age of our guests from the sixties to the forties. We now have a new customer base and we both think it was a terrific decision to build the spa. It was expensive – our spa cost £5 million to build, would you believe – and it's hard to see the return on our investment directly. But we transformed the business from fuddy-duddy to modern, and secured it for the next twenty years. Hotels that don't move with the times will find that their business won't last. You need to keep ahead of the curve.

We were doing very well, I'm pleased to say, all the way through the 1990s and 2000s, and then, of course, 2008 came and the world changed. The Park Hotel Kenmare suffered a substantial drop in turnover, from which we've never fully recovered. This is in part because Dublin hotels are charging silly prices and we can't charge four times more because people will view it as poor value for money and they won't come. So we've had to adjust accordingly. We've dropped our rates hugely, so we have no money for redevelopment. But that's the way it is – we're not alone in this. Like many Irish businesses, we've suffered, but what other option is there but to keep going?

Resilience is key in my business, and openness to fresh ways of thinking. In fact, I think openness is key in any walk of life. We can all get 'tunnel vision' sometimes, and we can forget that there are other approaches to life, other ways of looking at things. That's why I've always tried to keep myself open to new opportunities, because I know they'll broaden my horizons and make me look at my own life in a new way. And that's what I'm going to talk about next!

—

Have you tried anything new today?
It doesn't have to be something big
– just take a different route to work,
or walk instead of driving. Read
a book instead of the paper or have
a mocha instead of a latte. Go for
a swim instead of watching TV, or
see a movie – what's stopping you?
Only yourself!

5.

Living
in the
Limelight

> *'The talent of success is nothing more than doing
> what you can do well, and doing well whatever
> you do without thought of fame.'*
> Henry Wadsworth Longfellow

I've often felt that life is so much about luck and chance. You can be just going along, happy as Larry, and then something will come along to take you out of your normal routine. For me, that was my work in the media. Now, while I'm still very much a hotelier who works in TV, rather than the other way around, I consider that I've been very lucky to have had some terrific opportunities and to have been at the stage of life where I was able to make the most of them. If I'd been approached to do something like *At Your Service* while I was just starting off at the Park Hotel Kenmare, I'd have had to say no, but I'm a great believer in things happening for a reason and the media career came along just at the right time for me.

I'm something of an accidental media person, however. You probably won't believe it, but I was never really a 'performer' at school – it was my brother, Damien, who was the theatrical one. He'd have been in charge of our little plays when we were children and, even now, back in Sligo, he is still treading the boards with his Yeats Experience. I know that people call me flamboyant, but I am honestly not aware of it – it's simply who I am and I suppose I'm fortunate that that comes across well on television. But as a young man I was probably too practical by nature and too eager to get on with life. As I said, I was a late bloomer!

My first media appearance was at Dublin Zoo when I was aged two, and, no, not in an enclosure! Like many Dublin families at the time, a visit to the Zoo was a great treat for us and a rare one – we only went a handful of times in my childhood, and on one of these occasions a photographer – I think it was Edmund Ross – had taken a photo of me in my pushchair. When, aged nine, I returned to the zoo, there I was up on the wall in the visitor's centre. A friend of ours, Pauline Austin, who was a great knitter and who worked in John Lewis, London, had made me a great knitted coat and hat and I looked very smart. I like to say I was an attraction!

My current media career started one night in 2006, when I was watching the RTÉ *News*. At the end of the bulletin, there was an ad for a brand new architectural show, *Designs for Life*. It was a six-part show, and each week they'd take a different renovation project and see it through to completion. I sat up and thought, Oh, this could be interesting, because, twenty years before, I'd bought this little Victorian cottage in a row in Kenmare and I hadn't been able to do it up properly. I liked the idea of working with an architect and doing it well – if you are going to do something, do it right, I say! So, I grabbed a pencil and wrote down the name of the production company, Stopwatch Productions, and sent off an A4 sheet with details of the house and my plans for it. At the time, I had plans to turn it into a lovely bachelor pad for my retirement, and as some of the other cottages on the street were very run down, I thought it might regenerate the street.

I didn't hear anything for a while and then, on the June bank holiday of that year, I got a letter telling me that I was in the final twenty projects under consideration for the show and asking me if I was still interested. A lovely man called Tom Murphy from Stopwatch came down to see me and I had a little camera test. He sat behind the camera and asked me thirty questions, which I answered. It seemed to go okay

– he didn't run away screaming, anyway! I felt nervous at the start, because I'd never been in front of a TV camera before, but I soon began to relax.

Tom explained the concept behind the show, that it would follow the progress of my renovation project from planning to the final home, and that the show would pay for the architect and I'd pay for the renovations. It sounded perfect, and then he told me that the architect would be Rory Murphy, then of Studio M architects.

The name sounded familiar and then I remembered why – he was a protégé of a world-famous architect named Jean Nouvel, who had designed the Guthrie Theater in Minneapolis; if you haven't seen it, Google it – it's spectacular. It has a bridge that leads down to the Mississippi River and the cladding lights up at night to display images from productions. Now, I remembered Jean Nouvel's name well, because Joe Dowling, my great friend, was running the theatre at the time it was revamped in the mid-2000s (2015 was his last season as artistic director). The theatre was to be totally rebuilt, courtesy of the Pillsbury family, of Pillsbury Doughboy fame, at a cost of $125 million. And the finished project was stunning. However, there was only one slight problem – nobody could see anything! The lights in the foyer had been installed at great cost, following Jean Nouvel's instructions, but were impossibly gloomy, and so Siobhán, Joe's wife, insisted that they be put up to 60 watts. Of course, when the architect arrived for the opening, he nearly had a heart attack! So, having been invited to the opening myself, I managed to insert myself beside the great Jean Nouvel, who was fuming, and distract him with a stream of chatter. I always tell Joe that I saved him from Jean Nouvel! But, quite honestly, you couldn't have eighty-year-old Midwesterners tripping and breaking their necks. Form and function needed to come together!

I wasn't a bit put off by the Nouvel connection and so off we went, Rory and I, and he provided a beautiful design for the house. He really worked sympathetically with the age of the cottage, but the design was very modern at the same time. I was only delighted, until I bumped into one of my neighbours one morning. 'Do you know that the front wall [of the house] will fall down when you take the roof off? he warned me. I didn't pay much heed. The roof came off and all was well until August, when, after a few weeks' good weather, the wall fell down! By this stage, the project had taken on a life of its own – when we'd cleared the garden we discovered that we had a much bigger site than we'd thought, which gave us room to put on a nice extension.

Oh, well, we thought, we'll simply have to rebuild the wall. But, just to be on the safe side, I decided we'd need to record it all with the planner. Except that the planner didn't exactly see things our way. It turned out that, as we were building a new wall, and the plans didn't include a new wall, we had to ask for planning permission. In the meantime, we had to close the site, which duly flooded after being untouched for seven months. I was disappointed and frustrated, but recognised we had to do it the right way or not at all. It was a very stressful experience, I have to say, more stressful than any renovations I ever did at the Park Hotel Kenmare. I think when something is 'your own', you do become emotionally involved in it and it's hard to step away.

Between the jigs and the reels, my house actually took three and a half years to complete, and it's lovely, but you can imagine how difficult it would be to make a TV show if every project took three and a half years! Eventually, only four out of the six shows were made, and I really felt for the production company because it was a brilliant idea and everybody loved the show.

I thought that was pretty much it for my career in media, but then a lady called Gráinne MacAleer from RTÉ came to Waddell Media with an idea for a programme, and because they'd liked me on *Designs for Life*, they contacted the Park Hotel Kenmare to meet up with me. At this stage, in 2006, I was up to my eyes at the hotel and media work was the last thing on my mind, but my brother John, who knows me better than I know myself, had other ideas. John is always organising things for me, and it drives me mad, but I suppose I have him to thank for my media career!

It had been a busy day at the hotel and I came down to reception to find John there. 'I got you a TV show,' said he. 'I told them you'd love to do it.'

I thought I'd misheard him. 'I'd love to do what?'

'A TV show. It's made for you,' he said. 'You go into hotels and B&Bs and you critique them to see if they can be improved.'

'I'm not doing it,' I shot back. It didn't sound like something for me at all – who was I to be going around criticising other people's businesses? 'No way,' I said. But what is it Eleanor Roosevelt said – 'Do one thing every day that scares you'? I started thinking about that ... and the prospect of the show certainly scared me! And then word came back that Waddell Media were very disappointed that I'd said no, and they were sending the Managing Director Jannine Waddell down to the Park Hotel Kenmare to see me. RTÉ would only do the show if it was with me, so Jannine needed to work her magic.

I was persuaded to do a test shoot at a local friend's B&B, having been assured that it wouldn't be broadcast – 'It's just a dummy run.' Good job, I thought, because I'm not doing this. Eight series later and I'm still here! The show regularly brings in more than half a million viewers and, John tells me, is number three in the viewing figures after *Fair City* and *Love/Hate*. I like to think this an example to everybody who's getting older – if an aul' fella like me can take on such a challenge, anyone can!

There's no secret to *At Your Service* – no hidden planning or any behind-the-scenes rehearsing. Waddell Media seek applications for people to appear on the show, and they get a lot of them, not all of whom are suitable for our needs: the businesses may be too small or unsuitable in other ways. So, when Waddell whittle the list down to about twenty candidates, they send their profiles to John and me. Now, we began the show with hotels and B&Bs, and we still visit those businesses, but recently we've expanded a bit into golf clubs, a barge business, horses – all tourism-related businesses, but a step outside the usual.

The next stage in the process is that Waddell send somebody out to the candidate's business with a small camera to film them. You really don't know if people can 'do' camera until you try it; sometimes people get absolutely camera shy and turn to jelly! We have to be sure that they'll be comfortable talking and moving around in front of a camera. I learned that lesson myself when I did *Designs for Life* – I didn't know that I was going to be good at being on camera, but I just was. I learned that I had a natural manner and was an animated speaker. So Waddell go off and film the dozen or so places and send the CDs – the 'rushes', as they call them – back to John and me and we review them to see if the business has potential and the people have a bit of character and are relaxed on camera. And sometimes people we select decide they don't want to do it, which is fine.

Eight businesses are chosen from that process, and then Waddell put the schedule together for filming the series. Each show will take five days of us filming on site, and, if any refurbishment needs to be filmed, we send a small camera team down to do that. Then John and I do our filming and this is edited back up in Belfast with Waddell.

Richard Weller was our original series producer/director, followed by the lovely Maggi Gibson, who has been with the series almost as long as I have. We are completely on each other's wavelength: she knows how I think and I know how she thinks. Most of our camerawork has been done by Ken O'Mahoney, one of Ireland's finest cameramen – he really has a brilliant eye – and Finnie Byrne, Hugh Fox and Kevin McCarthy are on sound. We have a tight crew and have had the same people all through the years, which helps with the production and the way the programme is presented. And I know what the crew want me to do in terms of the camera and the light.

It's very complex, camera shooting, so I've had to learn a lot. It is a one-camera shoot, so there can be quite a lot of repetition for me as the presenter. I'll do a piece with the camera in front of me, and I'm talking to it, but then, at some stage, Ken will need to take a shot of me from the back, say, so I'll have to repeat what I said, but, more importantly, I will have to repeat the same movements, remembering what hand I opened the door with, which hand I had the suitcase in, etc. As another example, I might do interviews with the clients with the camera behind my shoulder and pointed at the client, and then we reverse and they have to call out the answers to questions that I've already asked with the camera pointing at me, nodding away! Continuity is very important. I've also learned that lighting is very complicated – you can look yellow if the light is wrong or if there is too-bright sunlight – and sound is also critical. Wind is our worst enemy, and by that I mean the meteorological kind! It can make an awful 'whooshing' sound over the microphone in outdoor shots.

On camera, they are always looking for 'the surprise', something exciting to liven up the story. I remember once we were doing a show in the Enable Ireland facility in Sandyford Industrial Estate, and we were knocking down plasterboard walls. I was banging away with my sledgehammer on camera, trying to get the wall to go down, but I wasn't strong enough, and then the nice Polish builder hit the wall just once and it went flying. So, back on camera I went, and I was working away pretending to hammer when the roof fell on top of me. It looked brilliant on camera, even though I was nearly killed!

Some people think that there's a lot of pre-planning and rehearsal for the way I arrive at the business in question, but I can assure you there's not. I simply turn up on the first day to whatever place I'm visiting and I have no idea at all what's behind the door. I'll have seen the rushes with the people I'm visiting and maybe an exterior shot or two of the place, but nothing else. I'm not allowed in until the cameras are rolling, because that way I'm genuinely surprised at what I see. Sometimes shocked!

I freely admit that I have an eye for detail in this area because of my father's 'tidy' genes, and after so many years at the Park Hotel Kenmare – I think I'd be called 'detail-oriented'! And in the hotel business small details really matter. The moment I go into a business, I'm able to spot things, and not just the obvious things, like dated furnishings or mouldy carpets. Recently, I was in a high-end boutique on Bleecker Street, New York, promoting the Park Hotel Kenmare, and within five minutes I'd spotted that the air conditioning vent was turned the wrong way around, so chilly air was pouring in over the clients, and it was unbelievably noisy, due to all the hard surfaces – the place needed a carpet or curtains. I see what's wrong straight away. And I know that people often laugh at my 'toilet roll' habit, but I can tell you now – Francis Brennan knows what's what! This reputation came about when I visited one place and I noticed that the toilet roll was on the wrong way, pressed against the wall instead of the other way around. Now, there's only one way to hang toilet paper, because otherwise you use too many sheets when you're digging the spuds, so to speak – there is a method in my madness, you know!

But there's also a serious side to the programme and that is its role in helping people to improve their businesses. Many of the businesses that John and I look at for the programme experience similar issues: they've been inherited by a son or daughter who doesn't yet have the experience or the interest to run them; or they just haven't been maintained and now look tired and dated. It's hard to explain to people, particularly if they're operating on a shoestring, that you need to invest and upgrade constantly in the hotel industry, even just to maintain your business at its current level, never mind to grow it. The other thing is that very often the owners can have a bit of 'tunnel vision' about their business and are only interested in what they're doing, instead of getting out there and looking at other businesses and seeing what they can learn. John and I both find that travelling to other hotels to look at the latest innovations is essential to keeping our own business fresh and moving forward.

Over the course of eight series, John and I have been just about everywhere. We've travelled the length and breadth of the country, looking at all kinds of businesses, from seaside hotels to equestrian businesses, wedding venues to B&Bs – the lot. I've loved every minute of it because I love meeting people and hearing their stories, and I also love people who are trying to give it a go and make something work – often, all they need are a few more ideas and some steering in the right direction. And John and I have been happy to help and to offer our expertise, as well as to entertain the viewing public.

A few shows in particular stand out. I remember one lady in particular, Frances McDonogh, who had a B&B near Lough Key Forest Park in Roscommon, because she was just made for television. It was a lovely Victorian country house, but she wasn't making the most of it or of the proximity to the forest park ... and then there was the dance studio she was installing in the yard for her teenage daughter! But there was something about that lovely house and the warmth of Frances that set it apart. In Series 2, I went to the Portfinn Lodge Hotel – I remember this very fondly because of its spectacular location, in Leenane, Co. Mayo, and because it was a family business and I just love the idea of being able to help family businesses. I think they are prob-ably the most difficult, because family relationships and business don't go together as a rule. Business has to be quite neutral, I feel, and you can't really let emotion get in the way, and families are all about emotion! I know this sounds a bit strange as I work so closely with John, but I think we work well together because we complement each other in our working lives, as well as being brothers.

Many of the businesses I have visited that aren't on the obvious tourist trails really need a certain something to make them a destination place. People might be willing to stay in a less-than-fabulous B&B near the Cliffs of Moher, for example, because of the fantastic scenery, but if you have a business in a quieter county or location you have to work that much harder to bring in the visitors. So John and I would encourage these businesses to really focus on their unique selling points, or to develop some aspect of the business that would bring visitors to them. Of course, the whole area of eco-tourism has really taken off in recent years. John and I have visited Cloughjordan Ecovillage and also another lovely place called Glenribbeen Eco Lodge in Co. Waterford, both which provide 'eco-tourist' holidays. What surprised me about these two places, though, was that, eco issues apart, they were still in the business of providing good-quality hospitality.

As a businessman, I'm always surprised at how many of the owners have bought their guesthouse or hotel on a dream – because they've fallen in love with Dingle or Donegal and just have to live there, running a very time-consuming and expensive business while they're at it! I salute their energy, I really do, and John and I have had a great time knocking them into shape. They don't always take our advice, though – but advice is free, I always say.

Sometimes, if you're new to the business, you have ideas that aren't backed up by realistic principles. If a business is being refurbished, we always encourage the owner to open to a specific deadline, because cash flow is essential to new businesses. As an owner, you also have to be prepared to be there while the work is going on, to put your own personal stamp on things. And you have to pay attention to detail. It really is the little things that matter when it comes to hospitality, particularly if you are charging top dollar for the experience – that experience has to be worth it, down to the last little thing: the angle of the lampshades in the guest bedroom, the quality of the bed linen, the state of the carpets. I know it all costs money, but you'll make money in return. John and I are also firm believers in trying to make connections with other local enterprises. For example, if you run a hotel in a well-known fishing area, make sure that you offer fishing trips for the day, complete with rod licence; or if you have a business on the coast, see if there are any surfing/boating/fishing businesses that you can link with. The tourism business is all about connections.

At Your Service is not all about business, though. We've also done a number of specials in the not-for-profit sector. The Christmas 2010 special, an episode I remember with great fondness, was about Cappagh Orthopaedic Hospital. I became particularly emotional when I went back there, because I'd spent so much of my childhood in and out of the place and it holds a special place in my heart. So when we were asked by Cappagh Hospital Trust Manager John Dennehy to go in and do up two of the paediatric wards, we jumped at the chance.

When I went back, I was astonished to find that the hospital hadn't changed at all, even though it was absolutely spotless. Time had stood still in so many ways and it brought back a flood of memories. John and I set to work on refurbishing the wards, with special help from local businesses, and on providing a sensory garden, courtesy of local firm Donegan Landscaping. Maria Hunter of MH Interiors, Mallow, helped us with the specifics of getting companies to sponsor items we needed and also with the practicalities of design, such as bed design and design of the bedside lockers – so that you could actually reach them without falling out of bed! The building work was done for free by the Cappagh Hospital contractors. The garden in particular was beautiful, full of lovely bright colours and sculpture, and of course it was wheelchair accessible. The two new wards opened in 2011, and quite honestly I was moved to tears by the whole thing and by understanding how much my parents sacrificed while I was there.

Now I'm on the board of Cappagh Hospital Trust and I'm delighted to be able to give back. In 2015, the hospital organised a sponsored walk along the Camino de Santiago, and even though I couldn't walk the whole thing because of my foot, I was there to lead the groups into and out of some of the towns along the way.

Our second special took in the Enable Ireland Centre in Sandymount, Dublin, and our brief was to improve the visitor centre there. I have to say, it's a fantastic facility, with a swimming pool, a garden centre and a workshop that makes brilliant orthopaedic chairs, but it had all gotten a bit run down and was in an unappealing breezeblock grey. We had three weeks to turn it around. First, we visited Newlands Garden Centre, which has won all kinds of awards, to get a look at best practice, and then we went to the fabulous Arboretum Garden Centre in Carlow, which has seven different gardens on display and a gorgeous restaurant. The Enable Ireland staff were full of enthusiasm and we really brightened up the garden centre.

Our third special was set in CASA respite centre in Malahide, Dublin. CASA organise events for people with intellectual disabilities, including social meetings and trips to Lourdes, and also have facilities in their lovely respite centre, the Breakhouse, which, at the time, needed a little TLC. It had originally been built in the 1970s and needed refurbishing. On the first morning, we turned up to take a look at the house at 7.15 a.m., and there was a great big fellow with a Munster jersey removing the windows! The owner of a well-known joinery firm, Munster Joinery, had heard about the show on *The John Murray Show* and had donated all the windows for the house free of charge, plus the labour to install them. This man wished to remain anonymous, but I wrote to thank him. In addition to refurbishing the Breakhouse, Brown Thomas kindly offered its services to help CASA with its shops in Clontarf and Phibsboro, advising about stock and merchandising.

I think these three specials will stay with me for ever, because I loved having the opportunity to do a bit of good. I think as a one-time 'service user', I have an appreciation of the amazing work that staff do in places like CASA, Enable Ireland and Cappagh.

At Your Service has also given me the opportunity to get involved in a lot of things that I might not have otherwise tried. I've suffered all kinds of indignities, but done some lovely things too, such as fishing in Shannon Harbour, falconry and golf, although no one would describe me as outdoorsy! I try to leave most of that kind of thing to John. I do remember being made to get on a horse at Crossogue House, Co. Tipperary, a lovely Georgian house and equestrian business. I had to learn to trot – bits of me moved that have never moved before or since! I was also meant to surf at Lahinch in Co. Clare for one programme, but I had to duck out because I'd broken three ribs earlier in the year – a lucky escape!

I feel incredibly lucky to have been involved in a fantastic series like *At Your Service*, and to have learned such a lot while being able to use my expertise as a hotelier. And I suppose the series changed my life, if that's not too much of an overstatement. I've been given all kinds of opportunities based on that show, some of which have been more successful than others, but that's TV and media for you. You never really know what's going to work and what's not. But I don't mind one little bit, because when you take chances in life you know some things will work out and some things won't, and so what? Nobody died, as a friend of mine always says.

Early in 2015, I was filming in Scarriff, Co. Clare. I was staying in the Lakeside Hotel in Killaloo. Ken, our cameraman, had gone off to take some exterior shots of the landscape and I went to my room. I put the key card into the slot and in I went. Now, the previous guests had left the television on, and what was flickering away on the screen but *Francis Brennan's Grand Tour* in Rome! It was very surreal.

If you are not familiar with the show, I had to take a group of people around various cities in Europe – Rome, Carcassonne, Barcelona, Tuscany, Cannes. What a nightmare, as you can imagine! Now, I've organised plenty of trips in my lifetime, but doing so for television is another matter altogether, and with a gang in tow ... sure, what could go wrong, as they say?

It hadn't quite started out like that. I had asked Waddell to see if they could get me a travel programme because I'm mad about travel, and I'd had an idea to do a kind of Fodor's Guide to a major city or historic site, like Rome or Venice. I wanted to do unusual things in those cities. But the way it works is that TV shows are commissioned as ideas and then presenters are attached to them, so I ended up on a bus with sixteen other people!

We did discuss the concept of the show over quite a long time – it took eighteen months to get to filming – but the show was slightly different from my expectations. We filmed it over ten days, which, considering we were visiting six cities, is at considerable speed. Perhaps that's why I seemed to spend all my time ushering people along! Also, in television, there are times when you have to redo the scene of the day because the director will have some idea in his or her mind about what will work. So I might have to don the clothes on Thursday that I'd worn on the Tuesday to retake the scene. Not a bother, even if, once, I had to change my clothes eleven times in the back of the bus, at 30 degrees Celsius. I know, you're probably not feeling that sorry for me, and you'd be right because we went to some very nice places and the people on the bus were lovely. It might have appeared, at times, that they were difficult, but they were just grand.

Now, I did have certain expressions that I used – 'Come on,' 'Hurry up,' 'You'll be late for the bus,' that kind of thing – and they did come back to haunt me! Believe it or not, the show wasn't filmed like that, but my catchphrases were played over and over as a kind of soundtrack and used as the hook. I don't have any issue at all with that, because it worked and that show is very popular, even though at times it might be hard to see myself in that way – it's hard for me to look at the show and think, That's me. On the other hand, how I'm portrayed on *At Your Service* is completely me.

I think, when it comes to television, it's nice to feel that I don't have to do anything I don't want to do. I only do TV because I enjoy it. My work was and still is the hotel business and that's who I am. However, television has really given me a boost and I've enjoyed every minute of it. I've often had some seat-of-the-pants experiences, mind you ...

I remember appearing on *The Restaurant* once, and straying a good bit from my comfort zone! I was due to be a judge on the show, which was being filmed in the Wineport Lodge in Athlone. I had been asked by Reg Looby, the producer. I was in the US at the time and I said that would be fine. What I didn't realise was that the chef they had booked for the show had had to cancel. The show had rung John at the Park Hotel Kenmare to ask if I'd be willing to be the chef, and of course John landed me in it by saying, 'Of course he will'! When I got back to Kenmare, exhausted after my trip, he said, 'Oh, by the way, you're cooking for the show. Just talk to the chef when you get back to the hotel and you'll be fine.' Needless to say, I nearly had a heart attack at the prospect of cooking for forty people. I am a perfectly okay home cook, but I'm not restaurant standard, I can tell you!

At the beginning of the week in which the show was to be filmed, I managed to get a menu together with the chef at the Park Hotel Kenmare that we thought would work, but between the jigs and the reels I didn't see him again for the rest of the week. So, by Sunday, as I drove up to the Wineport, I had a menu but nothing else! Now, when I got to Athlone, the production company put me up in a hotel and then drove me to the Wineport, because it's top secret who the mystery chef is. He or she is supposed to be a complete surprise and even the kitchen staff don't know. I was brought out to the restaurant and smuggled up to my room, where I proceeded to have a complete panic as I had no idea what I was going to do. And what's more, this show has four cameras on all the time, so every single move would be visible – there would be nowhere to hide!

On the appointed day, I was brought down to the kitchen to meet Stephen, the head chef, and the other staff, who were very nice, but I hardly had time to say hello when the director said, 'Right, let's get started!' I went over to my work station, where all the ingredients for my starter were laid out, and I looked at them blankly. What on earth would I do with the mountain of butter? There must have been eight pounds of it. The cameras were rolling and the sweat was rolling down my back. I decided I'd better do something and so I started chopping away as if everything was marvellous. I was making anchovy butter, apparently, to fill smoked salmon, but how on earth would I fit that mountain of butter into the mixer, I wondered.

'I'll just make up a small batch now,' I said brightly, and put some butter in the mixer. Then I went looking for the anchovies. The last time I'd seen an anchovy, it was brown, but the anchovies in the dish didn't look like any I'd ever seen, and now I really began to panic. I was praying that I didn't look as hot and sweaty as I felt, as I chattered away.

Then my assistant chef piped up, 'I'll get started on the risotto.'

'Off you go,' I said cheerfully, continuing to look busy with my anchovy butter. The next minute, I heard what I thought were hailstones behind me, and I turned to see him pouring the rice into the hot pan. 'What on earth are you doing?' I shouted.

'I'm making risotto,' he said calmly. 'You crack the dry rice on the hot pan and it absorbs the liquid much better.' I nodded as if I'd known that all along, and moved onto the main course, which was wild organic salmon and beef fillet. For the beef, you sear it on a really hot pan. Then you coat the fillet in ground coffee, paprika, garlic salt and plain salt and pop it in the oven. The coffee mix gives the beef a beautiful flavour. We used to have it in the hotel regularly and it was lovely.

I was searing away when the chef turned to me and said, 'What's the origin of that dish, now, Francis?' In the name of God, I thought, I haven't a clue! 'Oh, it's a South American dish,' I improvised. 'The steak comes from Argentina and the coffee from Colombia.'

I got four stars on *The Restaurant* that night and Paolo Tullio thought it was the nicest risotto he'd ever tasted since his mother's. How on earth I managed, I'll never know, but what I do know is that never, ever again will I cook on camera!

I got the chance to work outside my comfort zone again when I did this show called *Stars Go Racing*, where well-known people got involved with the horseracing world. I know, can you just see me? I turned up at the stables of this lovely woman called Joanna Morgan, a horse trainer and stud owner, who had been a very well-known jockey. I had never even been to a stables before, never mind sat on a horse – this was before my horse-riding exploits for *At Your Service*. But I'm never one to shirk hard work and so I found myself mucking out, tacking up and helping the riders up onto the horses – obviously, I wasn't allowed up on thoroughbreds myself! It did me the world of good, because I'm afraid of horses, dogs and other animals, and the place was coming down with them. When a horse put its head out of the stable doors, I remember saying, 'Now, don't spit on me,' before remembering that that's llamas or camels! And horses are strong, which I hadn't entirely understood before the programme. I'd be holding one by the reins and it would swing its head and nearly take my arm off! By the end of my stay, I was well able for them. I entered one of them in a race in Bellewstown, and it came second. I think Joanna was quite surprised that I turned out to be tougher than I looked; all that farm experience in Co. Sligo stood me in good stead.

When I think of myself ten years ago with my list of things I wanted to do in retirement, I can't believe that I've been lucky enough to do all that I have done. When I'm killed after a busy day's filming or I've been up at the crack of dawn for a week visiting businesses, I never think, 'Oh, I wish I wasn't doing this.' How could I wish not to have such opportunities? I feel truly blessed. I'd never have predicted that I'd be hosting a TV show with an audience of over half a million people, or that I'd be travelling the length and breadth of Ireland helping people to build their businesses. I'm a very lucky man. To come back to our happiness index in my introduction, I'm glad that I've tried something new – it's kept me young and stopped me getting stuck in my ways. What is it that fellow says in *Star Wars*? 'There is no try, only do.' I'm a firm believer in that.

People often ask me if I mind being recognised, and, sure, I don't mind a bit. I love meeting new people and getting new stories. And the thing I like the most is that, because *At Your Service* is a family show, young kids and teenagers come up to me to say hello when I'm out and about. And I don't mind a bit if people parody me – I consider it a compliment! The only time I find it a bit difficult is when I'm working away in the office at the hotel or having my dinner somewhere and someone wants a photo. Then I'll just politely ask the person if they can wait until I finish up what I'm doing or have eaten my main course. And no selfies – you can have a thousand pictures taken with me, but no selfies. I don't want to end up on the internet with a leprechaun hat and red trousers!

I've never entirely got used to the requests for photos when I'm at work, but I always try to oblige. Sometimes I'll tell the girls on reception I've got too much to do, and so they tell anyone who asks that I'm busy. I remember, one Sunday, the receptionist had gone for her tea so I was minding the front desk. A guest appeared at the desk and asked if he could have a photo. Caught, I had no option but to say, 'Yes, of course. I'd be delighted.' So, off we went, and we walked out under the canopy that extends from the front door, chatting away. I stayed put on the top step, knowing that that's where guests normally like to take the photo. All of a sudden, three ladies appeared. I assumed they were with the guest in question, so I ushered them up to the top step, one on my left and the other two on my right. I watched the gentleman position himself beside us and then it occurred to me: 'Who's taking the photograph?'

'You are,' he replied, looking confused as he handed me the camera. He had no idea who I was! He was an American and just wanted a photo of himself and his friends on the top step. Almost famous, I like to say!

I think my favourite 'fame' story, though, involves Pope Francis (but of course!). To explain, every year for the last five or six years we've worked with the cosmetics company Sisley, because we have a link with them in the US via Sámas, our spa. Now, it was February 2013, and we were in Santa Barbara, California, and my phone beeped. I looked at the message, which was from a friend; it said, 'Congratulations'. I wondered if I'd won the Lotto! My phone beeped again and there was another congratulatory text, which said, 'It's Francis!' I couldn't work out what my friends were on about, until one of the girls told me that Pope Francis had been elected that morning and my friends were all texting me in jest. Very funny, I thought. Ten minutes later, I received a text from the Park Hotel Kenmare, with a forwarded text a listener had sent into *The Ray D'Arcy Show*. This lady's seven-year-old was having his cornflakes at the breakfast table and there was a newsflash that there'd been white smoke in Rome and the new pope was ... Francis. The young fellow waved his spoon in the air and said, 'Hurray. It's that man from Kenmare!'

Whoever said that fame has a price wasn't totally right, I feel. To me, the price has been a small one, and pales in comparison to all the positives. I love this little quote from Abraham Lincoln: 'Don't worry when you are not recognised, but strive to be worthy of recognition.' That's what I try to do every day. Being well known is no good to me unless I can do something with it, and I've been able to use my profile to help the charities I've been working with, such as Breast Cancer Galway, Cappagh Hospital Trust, Kerry Diocese and Action Breast Cancer's Pink Ribbon campaign. I also enjoy visiting children with special needs as they seem to love the show. I've been able to do all kinds of things that I never would have expected to do, and I've been able to use my expertise in the job I love to help others. And if that isn't a recipe for happiness, I don't know what is.

As to the future, well, it probably won't look like the present. As you may know, John is stepping back from *At Your Service* because he sees himself first and foremost as a businessman and he has other projects in that area, such as continuing with his wedding/glamping business, Dromquinna Manor. And, quite honestly, John isn't as comfortable with being a public figure as I am. In fact, John became involved with the show almost by accident, because in the first series I used to phone him on camera for advice on the businesses

I visited and Waddell decided to bring him into the programme as it made for a better dynamic. And now I'm back on my own!

John's decision came about just after Christmas 2015. He and Gwen were on their way home from Dublin and they needed some candles so they stopped off in Cork. When they parked the car, John made to get out. 'Oh, no,' Gwen said. 'If you come, we'll be an hour and a half, and if I go on my own, I'll be in and out in ten minutes.' When she said, 'Oh, no,' he knew exactly what she meant and he decided that was that. He always said that if he got to the 'Oh no' stage, it was time to call a halt. I'll really miss John because we make such a good team. I can completely understand his decision, though, particularly as he has a family and I don't, so I know that no one else's privacy or comfort is at stake.

Another thing I'll need to consider is that, even though I've happily ignored my foot for most of my life, it has begun to give me a bit more trouble; I've had MRIs on it and on my back, and I have been told that I'll need to spend less time on my feet in the coming years. And so I might focus more on TV and media as there's less standing around than in the hotel. I have a few things sprouting, as they say, so watch this space.

——

Have you tried something
recently that's made you
nervous? Well, that would be
no bad thing. Try stepping
outside your comfort zone
and see what happens.

6.

Travel Broadens the Mind

> *'Travel makes one modest. You see what a tiny place*
> *you occupy in the world.'*
> Gustave Flaubert

I've always been a big traveller, not so I can come back and bore people with my photos and stories, but because I love to see other parts of the world and learn about other people. I truly believe that travelling helps you learn more about yourself as well as about the places and the people you are visiting. As Mark Twain said, 'Travel is fatal to prejudice, bigotry and narrow-mindedness.' I also think that, for me, it's something of an obsession. I am just hooked on the whole experience, not necessarily just the destination: I love the whole process of travelling. I spend a great deal of time in airports. I'd say I probably take anything up to forty-five flights a year. That's a lot, now that I come to think of it! I suppose airports are a little like hotels, so I feel at home, but I also love the little encounters with people that I have along the way. I also think that travel is a great outlet for me, because I don't have a family of my own and it's given me so much in terms of happy memories, as well as a close-knit group of friends who feel like family to me after all these years.

I first caught the travel bug as a teenager. I'd always been interested in travel as a young boy in Balally, but, like most Irish people at the time, we never went any further than this island. In my case, we went to Sligo to my mother's place. Then, when I was a teenager, my sister Kate and I were invited to a wedding in Paris. As you can imagine, this was the last word in those days, particularly for two teenagers from Dublin. The connection was Claire Wagram, the groom's sister, who had stayed with us in Balally for years as a student. Claire came from a very wealthy family. Her grandparents had manufactured the first espresso machines and they had an apartment with a full view of the Eiffel Tower. Claire used to love us, because we were a 'real' family who sat around the table and ate together and talked. She never wanted to go home.

For Kate and me, this was the trip of a lifetime. We stayed in a hotel for six nights, which was unheard of then unless you were part of the jet set, and the wedding was just unbelievable, like a feature in *Hello* magazine – our eyes were out on stalks for the entire week. Claire's brother was marrying a girl from Hawaii, and she had to convert to Catholicism, so she needed to be christened. And, naturally, they had a big party for the christening. Then she had to make her Confirmation, so there was another party, and then we had a rehearsal party the night before the wedding. Now, each party was in the Parisian equivalent of Dublin Castle. By the day of the wedding, we were exhausted from enjoying ourselves! The wedding itself was in the Bois de Boulogne in a private house and the guests were the cream of French society. I can still remember that the wedding cake was carried in by four chefs, and it was composed of fifteen different floating layers, raspberry and chocolate interleaved, and I was fascinated because it had no board underneath it; somehow, the cake had been engineered so it wouldn't fall apart – I couldn't work out how they'd done it. And, of course, the entertainment was top notch: there was a disco for the youngsters, a jazz room and an orchestra. We had never seen anything like it and we were only dying to tell our parents, but of course, in those days, you only phoned home in an emergency, so we had to keep it all to ourselves for a while.

I can also remember that Paris was where I discovered McDonald's. Now, I know that most people would remember the Jardins des Tuileries or Montmartre, but, remember, I always had an eye for business! It was only the early 1970s then, and fast food just didn't exist in Europe. I was mesmerised by this new concept. I brought home all the boxes and the packets and I still have every one of them in a file in the hotel – I don't throw anything away. As it happened, a short time later someone, probably a cousin, sent home an American newspaper and when I opened it, lo and behold, I saw an ad for McDonald's Corporation in it. I'm going to write to them, I thought, to see if I can get the franchise for Ireland. In my letter, I explained that I was a young student heading for catering college and I was very interested in taking on the franchise for Ireland. In fact, I was just a bit too late – it had already been taken up by a man in Naas, who held on to it until a few years later when the market was ready for fast food. But I like to think that I was far-sighted enough in my own mind to know that the Irish would love McDonald's.

After my Paris trip, my next adventure was backpacking, which, you can imagine, wasn't for me. I agreed to go with a few friends because I was at a rare loose end: I had just finished up in Marlin Communal Aerials and was waiting to go to college. I can still remember it, probably because it was so hugely unlike me (well, I have talked about trying new things!). I don't do that kind of thing, travelling around and staying in hostels; maybe this makes me sound a little bit of a snob, but it's not that actually. It's just that I like comfort and, in particular, I like to be able to book ahead; the free-and-easy, turn-up-on-the-night way of hostelling just makes me break out in a rash. And of course, this was long before smartphones and Google, so the whole process was even more hit and miss.

We started in Rosslare, catching the ferry to Le Havre, and then headed straight up to Norway because we wanted to do Scandinavia, but a sliced pan there was about £4, so we realised that we'd run out of money pretty quickly. The only thing I can remember about that part of the trip was that I was on a train in Uppsala, which was just pulling out of the station, and this man came running up the platform and just caught it in time. He sat down beside me and I thought, Oh, he doesn't look well, and the next thing he slid down the seat. I ran up and down the train looking for help. I found two soldiers, who performed CPR, but I don't think the poor man survived. We got an awful fright, I can tell you. Matters didn't really improve in Chur in Switzerland, where some people's wallets were robbed, even though, like our fellow residents in the dorm, we'd put them in our pillowcases at night. Somehow, the robber had managed to slit the pillowcases with a knife and rob a ton of wallets. Even though I escaped, it didn't exactly alter my opinion of backpacking. I survived it, but I wasn't made to rough it, clearly!

'The man who goes alone can start today; but he who travels with another must wait till that other is ready.' Now, this little quote by Henry David Thoreau sums up my travels in later life with my great friends in Skål, a professional organisation for people in the tourist industry. For me, that's one of the great pleasures of travel: doing it with other people.

The organisation has AGMs all over the world – Cairns, Mombasa, New York – and I began to attend conferences in the late 1970s. Eventually, a group of about twenty of us from Ireland began to holiday prior to or after the conference, which normally took place at the end of the hotel season. We became great friends, even though, sadly, there are only nine of us left now. I was very much the baby of the group – they call me 'the kid' – and the others are now in their eighties and nineties, but we've always gotten on like a house on fire because we are all on each other's wavelength, in spite of the age difference. And, most importantly, when we travel we split everything evenly, so there are no rows. We also have similar ideas about what we like to do on holiday and where we like to go. And we have a laugh, we really do.

I have to say, though, that enjoying travel really depends on having this happy dynamic, as the one time that we didn't we really regretted it. We were going to South America, I remember, because our 1997 conference was in Rio. I'd always wanted to go down the Amazon, so I was really looking forward to the adventure. And then Mary, a lovely member of the group from Galway, rang and said that her two friends Penelope and Cyril from England wanted to come with us.

Now, my memories of Penelope from a previous encounter at a Skål conference were that she wore a 1930s frilly dress and open-toed sandals at all times and was very parsimonious, and he was the same. It didn't bode well.

'Mary,' I said gently, 'I'm not sure that's a great idea ...'

'Not at all,' she said. 'It'll be grand altogether. Don't worry!'

'Mary,' I said, 'they could be tricky.'

'No, no, it'll be fine,' she insisted, so with great foreboding, I went along with it. I have to say, I didn't know either Cyril or Penelope that well because I'd only ever met them at conferences, where you'd just make small talk – 'Oh, hello, how are things in Norwich?' that kind of thing – and it's not as if you really care; it's all just chat. But to spend a fortnight with them in the jungle? I really had my doubts. I know what Mark Twain said about travel being an antidote to prejudice, but I wasn't so sure it would alter my prejudice in Cyril and Penelope's case!

Anyway, off we went to the rainforest in Manaus, which you might know as the place of Teatro Amazonas, a Renaissance-style opera house which just appears in the middle of the jungle. It was in the film *Fitzcarraldo*, and apparently Caruso sang there.

In our group, we have certain unwritten rules. For a start, nobody worries about money and how it's spent: one day Mary will buy the coffees and the next day I will, and so on. And it's not because people might be better off; there's just an understanding that everyone takes a turn. And the great thing is that there's no fighting over money: if one person wants to take a tour and the other doesn't, the first person will pay for the tour that day; someone else will pay to see an attraction the next day, and so on. It's never an issue. And when we all go out to dinner, I'm always in charge – I'd be a bit controlling like that, but everyone appreciates it because it means they don't have to work things out themselves. Of course, I don't drink, but I pay an equal share every night and then, on the last night, the group buys me dinner. I'm as happy as Larry, because they acknowledge the fact that I don't drink.

So, on this particular night in Manaus, we were in a restaurant and along came the bill. I always add a 10 per cent tip and then divide it by the number of people at the table, so I called down, 'Okay, everybody, forty-two dollars each. Send it up.' Everybody rummaged around for their money, but then I heard the sound of throat clearing down the back. It was Cyril.

'How can it be forty-two dollars?' he said. 'Penelope didn't have any dessert and neither did I.'

I said, 'Cyril, we've been travelling together for nineteen years and this is the way we do it. But if you don't want to dine with us any other evening, we don't mind at all.' There's nothing I find more irritating than a person not willing to pay their fair share. I'm not taking that for a ten-day holiday, I thought. As it happened, Cyril and Penelope didn't eat with us the next night! It didn't bother me because I felt that the rule of the group needed to be respected.

I had booked a big adventure for the group the following day. We were to go on a steam paddleboat up the Amazon, where we'd stay for a couple of nights in little cabanas run by the indigenous people, who are pygmies. Now, the Amazon is made up of tributaries. There's the Negro, so called because it's been stained a kind of tea colour by all the vegetation, and the Branco, which comes from the frozen snow of the Andes. At one particular point, the two currents flow side by side down river for eight miles before they merge, black on one side and white on the other – you can see them from space or on Google Street View, believe it or not!

Everything was going beautifully. We were all admiring the views and the river, and after a while our paddle steamer came to a halt. It was time to get into the canoes, which were waiting by the river bank to take us to our destination, each with two pygmy gentlemen in charge. How do we get down there? I thought, whereupon the captain dropped anchor and then threw a rope ladder, World War 2-style, over the side of the boat. Oh my God, I thought, how on earth will we manage that? None of us was exactly young and one of the party had MS; as we tried to lower him into this tiny canoe I wondered if we were out of our minds.

Our hosts didn't speak a word of English, but they indicated that they'd like four people in each boat. After everyone else had clambered down the ladder, I was left with Cyril and Penelope. As I was going over the side, Cyril said, 'When I get into the pygmy boat, I'm not getting out.' He had a panicked look on his face.

'Why not?' I was getting a bit impatient now, hanging, as I was, off the side of the boat.

'I read about it. You can't get into the water in the tributaries of the Amazon because there are these little worms and they go up ...' And here he pointed to his nether regions.

I said, 'Cyril, nothing will go up there, I promise.' I didn't mention the piranhas!

We clambered aboard the canoes, Penelope in her 1930s flowery dress and her hat that looked as if it came from the Anzac Museum of sheep herding, and Cyril, huffing and puffing away, and off we went up a tributary of the river. There was blissful silence for a moment as we took in the view and then eagle-eye here saw the canoe way up the front stopping and then much pushing and shoving – the Amazon has a lot of sandbanks, so sometimes there's no choice but to climb out and push.

Our hosts asked us to get out, and I duly obliged.

Cyril said, 'I'm not getting out.'

'But the man says you have to get out,' I said, exasperated.

'No, no, Penelope and I aren't getting out,' he insisted. Those blessed river worms again! The heat was absolutely sweltering, and here I was with two pygmy gentlemen pushing a 20-stone Englishman and his wife in her floral dress over the sandbank. I thought I'd kill them.

Eventually, we got over the sandbank and paddled along the river until we got to the village. A Swiss man had built the cabanas, and they were quaint, but basic. There was no electricity and the 'shower' was the udder of a cow! You pulled a rope and the udder gushed water all over you. Very ingenious. Now, the place was alive with wildlife and I have to admit I was terrified at night, with insects and God knows what else scurrying everywhere, but it was a real experience and great fun.

When I travel, I have to admit that I'm fussy about my food and always careful about what I eat, because I don't want to get sick – I always eat fruit that can be peeled, that kind of thing – and so I skipped the spaghetti Bolognese that was on offer for dinner. But, lo and behold, Cyril and Penelope tucked in! They both had a big helping of spag. Bol. and next day they were both dying, in a shocking state. I had tablets with me and I left them with poor Cyril, and then off I went on a rainforest walk, led by the locals, to look at all the different plants, which was just fascinating. They showed us what they use for the poison at the tip of their arrows and for medicines; the pygmies suffer a lot because they live in such damp conditions, and sadly they often die quite young, of pulmonary conditions and that kind of thing quite young. The life expectancy is only forty. I can't imagine what it must be like to live in this wonderful place that's teeming with life, but that requires non-stop work and effort just to survive. It's a hard life. I also vividly remember on that trip that we went fishing for piranhas. I couldn't believe that they were leaping and jumping out of the water. I thought they'd eat the leg off me, but when we caught them and roasted them they were very nice, like perch. I don't think it'll be on the menu of the Park Hotel Kenmare any time soon, but it was great to try something new!

When I came back from my rainforest walk, himself was sitting on the porch.

'How are you feeling, Cyril?' I asked. 'Did you take the tablets?' Now, the tablets were the size of the head of a pin, but what does he say?

'They were too big to swallow.'

I lost my patience a bit then and said, 'You could have shoved it up the other end!' That wasn't nice, but I'm afraid Cyril exhausted every bit of Christian patience I possessed. Then he wanted to know if he could get a refund because he didn't go on the walk. Do you know, we've never invited anyone outside the group to come with us on our travels since. I wonder why!

When I've travelled, I've had to get used to odd people, but I've also had to be a bit ingenious about working things out for myself. If you travel you have to be prepared to be re-sourceful, because in a foreign place there's no point in hiding away. I get a great sense of satisfaction from finding my own way around; it makes me feel like a local. And on one occasion in Thailand, all my resourcefulness was tested to the limit.

I had gone to Thailand for a Skål conference, holidaying with the gang in Phuket after, which was lovely. After the gang had gone home, I headed for Hua Hin, where a friend of mine, Dan Mullane, had an apartment, which he was lending me for a week. Now, if you don't know Hua Hin, it's one of those paradise spots with sandy beaches like icing sugar and thick green vegetation, but because it's not too far from Bangkok it's a bustling kind of place, with lots of markets. It was actually a getaway for the Thai royal family for many years, and one of the palaces is still occupied by the royal family. It's called Far From Worries Palace, which I like the sound of!

I rented a car to get to Hua Hin, which was a task in itself because the car was in among about fifty others and I had to perform feats of spatial awareness to get it out, moving one car back and then another forward, a car left then a car right, until finally I got my car out and was able to drive away. It was like a Rubik's Cube of automobiles! And then there was the driving. I thought, as a lunatic driver myself, I'd fit in, but the locals showed me how it was really done, with four-ton lorries passing me on the inside. I arrived in Hua Hin eventually, sweat pouring off me, and tried to decipher Dan's directions, which were scant to say the least. The town is bisected by a motorway, so you can't cross it easily, so I had to go about twenty miles out of my way – it felt like that anyway – to turn left and come back to try to find the apartments. Then I spotted the lovely Hotel Chiva-Som and I thought I'd ask there because I knew the owners. They explained that the apartments were quite a way out of town.

Off I went again in my little car. I was in the middle of nowhere, it was getting dark and there wasn't a light to be seen, so I pulled over and looked at Dan's directions again. I did remember he'd mentioned a railroad and I'd seen a sign for one a while back. I went and turned left, and ended up on a hippy beach and I thought, No! And then I came upon a multi-storey building, which loomed up out of nowhere. Aha, I thought, this looks promising. I parked and went inside, and when I didn't spot anyone at reception, called out 'Hello!' And three men popped up from behind the counter, drunk as lords.

The poor men didn't speak any English, so couldn't understand my questions, but one of them led me through the myriad of buildings and I ended up in an office, where there was a another man watching TV, feet propped up in front of him. He didn't seem to know Dan Mullane, but then the colour-coded keys hanging on the wall caught my eye. 'Do you have a name for the owners of these keys?' I asked, hoping that there would be a list of people. Yes, he had a book and when I looked through it, there it was, 'Mullanes'.

My drunk friend was only delighted to bring my bags to the apartment and so up we went. Dan had told me that it was very sparsely furnished, because he'd only recently bought it. In we went and my friend jumped up on the sink and began to flick the switches in the fuse box to turn the electricity on. Meanwhile, I looked around and I saw a beautiful apartment, with sofas and coffee tables and glossy magazines. It didn't look like I'd imagined from Dan's description. Then I went over and opened the bedroom door... to find two people fast asleep in bed! I nearly had a stroke. I closed the door very quietly and urged my friend to be quiet. 'Get out,' I whispered, making flapping motions with my hand, ushering him out the door.

It turned out, from his scant instructions, that Dan had indeed directed me to apartment 521, except he'd forgotten that he lived in 512! Later, when I rang Dan to remonstrate with him, he laughed and laughed, 'Sure, didn't you find it in the end?' I suppose I did find it, through my own ingenuity, and I did have a lovely week there, but the holiday was to provide one more adventure on the way back, once more of the driving variety.

On the day I was flying home, I left Dan's apartment very early to allow for any traffic disasters and because I needed to get petrol. I pulled into a garage and after I'd filled the tank I asked three lads on bikes for directions to the airport, because the signs are in Thai, reasonably enough, and it can be hard to know where you're going. The young lads didn't speak English, so I had to resort to charades, miming an aeroplane and making suitable noises.

Oh, yes, they could direct me to the airport, but from what they told me, in a mixture of broken English and sign language, it seemed there was a short cut. Two highways ran parallel to each other and at one stage they were within a few feet of each other, even if one was about two feet higher up than the other. The long way meant following one highway until there was a junction that led to the other. The short way meant spotting a gap in the wall between the two, which the locals had helpfully created by knocking a hole in that wall, and making the leap, at top speed, up to the other highway, saving yourself two hours in the process. It was like Cirque du Soleil!

I took off from the petrol station in my car with my instructions to be alert at the thirty kilometre mark, where I'd see the gap in the wall. So I was watching and waiting; 20, 25 kilometres went by, and, lo and behold, there was my hole in the wall. I had about 30 feet to get from highway A to highway B, so I picked up speed and off I went, making the leap onto the other highway and zooming off to the airport. I was delighted with myself – *Fast and Furious* had nothing on me!

I've been to many places, but I think some of my best memories come from my trips to Mexico, and in particular to a wonderful central Mexican city called San Miguel de Allende. It's a long way from Acapulco and places like that, but it has charm and tons of wonderful Spanish architecture – it's actually a UNESCO world heritage site and full of atmosphere. However, all the surprises aren't visible immediately; they are hidden behind huge wooden double doors that line the narrow streets. Each of these doors – wide enough to take a horse and carriage through – opened into a cobbled courtyard surrounded by a colourful nineteenth-century house. Many of the houses behind these wonderful porticos have now been lovingly restored.

The people of the town used to be 100 per cent farming stock, but now tourism plays a huge part in the local economy. As luck would have it, the day we arrived for our Small Luxury Hotels of the World (SLHW) conference coincided with the town's saint's day and the place was bustling with activity. Now, being Mexico, where nothing is as you might expect it, the festivities were to kick off at four o'clock in the morning. Yours truly, not wanting to miss anything, as it might have been my last time there, wanted to see how the locals would celebrate their 'St Patrick's Day', as it were, and I looked for volunteers among my friends to join me. I ended up with five out of the twelve, which wasn't bad.

Of course, as a teetotaller, I didn't join the gang after dinner for drinks downtown (I also knew I'd be setting my alarm for 3.30 the following morning), instead going for a quick walk before bed to get my bearings. Now, the square is always the place of action in Mexican towns so I headed down there. Well, it was like an All-Ireland match day and the Super Bowl rolled into one; the only difference was that the assembled masses were the poorest people one could ever meet.

As I stood in the throngs, I realised that the whole of the surrounding hinterland must come into town for the festivities. Not being able to speak Spanish, I wasn't able to ask what the huge construction was in front of the church, but it looked to me like a huge bamboo model of Gulliver in Lilliput. I couldn't work out what it might be for, but it looked promising!

Drink seemed to be the first priority of the night and so I left well enough alone and off I went to bed at 11.00 p.m. The following morning, when I arrived down to the foyer in the small hours it was to find that my friends were only just returning from their night out after a few Coronas! They were all under the weather, and so yours truly had to set out alone and sober for the event.

Now, as you can imagine, I spend quite a bit of time alone and sober when travelling with the gang, but I don't mind – it means I see all kinds of things that they miss – but I do remember one trip to Sydney Harbour Bridge had to be called off because sobriety was an issue and I'm still raging! To explain, we had booked a trip to climb the bridge, which was to be a real highlight of our stay in Sydney, but for safety reasons only twelve could go – you have to wear a harness and that kind of thing. As there were thirteen of us, I fell on my sword and opted to stay at home, but, what do you know, they stayed out all night and when the appointed time came they were all too 'under the weather' to attempt the thing. I haven't entirely forgiven them.

Anyway, back to San Miguel. Now, at 4.00 a.m. the square was absolutely packed, and everyone seemed to be drunk, men women and children! Of course, I'm exaggerating, but there was a general air of carefree abandon. Events started promptly. I have to say, I was a bit surprised at this northern European-style promptness, but then I learned that the local priest is in charge of the whole thing, and because he has such a huge workload he tries to make sure it all goes off on time. There was a kind of *Riverdance* show, Mexican style, with lots of singing and dancing, and then it came time to light a fire under my Gulliver in Lilliput. I later learned that all of the large towns in Mexico have their own saint's day, and fireworks are the order of the day, as each town tries to outdo the other for sheer spectacle; my bamboo Gulliver was San Miguel's salvo in the ongoing war. And it wasn't Gulliver, but Christ!

I had taken shelter under the arches of the colonnade on the square, and I watched as a huge firework was lit at his toe and erupted in a kind of spiral sequence up legs, arms and torso. I was lucky that I'd selected this hiding place, because showers of sparks shot out over the masses as the fireworks zoomed and cracked and the spiral went up the body of Jesus. When it got to his waist, the crown of thorns on his head began to revolve slowly, picking up speed until it was revolving wildly, like one of Amelia Earhart's aeroplane propellers, and then it took off into the sky! What a spectacle, I thought; entertaining, if not exactly reverent.

The next day, I was out and about and happened across half of the town sporting newly applied bandages on heads and eyes, which I thought was interesting. When I got back to the hotel, I fell into conversation with the receptionist, who told me that it was a great honour to be hit by a falling firework, as it signalled that you would have great luck in life. I can only imagine what it might mean to be hit by the crown of thorns – it would probably guarantee entry to heaven! Personally, I was more inclined to stick with the three Hail Marys.

San Miguel was such a marvellous place, but I remember that getting there was a bit of a task. We'd been staying in Mexico City at a hotel called the Marquis Reforma, which was run by a man called Jose Kalach, a member of the board of Small Luxury Hotels of the World. We had to go to San

Miguel for our board meeting, simply because the hotel there hadn't paid its fees to the organisation and the meeting was a quid pro quo – a lucky eventuality, I have to say, and I feel blessed to have had the chance to go there.

Anyway, on the day of our departure to San Miguel, I had to whip the gang into shape to get them all going, and I marshalled them down the steps of the hotel to the waiting VW bus, which seemed to be accompanied by a number of men in military dress with automatic weapons. I assumed that there must be some visiting dignitary around – a president from a junta or two.

The gang assembled, chatting, at the top of the steps, ignoring the armed forces, and I had to shuffle them all down the steps to the bus, whereupon a Mercedes 500 pulled up in front of the bus, and the doors opened. Great, I thought, as I tucked them all into the bus, I'm going to see a junta leader in the flesh. By this stage, the bus was full and I was wondering where I was going to sit, when Jose came running down the steps. 'Quick, get in,' he said.

'But there's no room,' I protested, indicating the bus.

'Get into the Merc,' he said, as if I was a total eejit – whereupon I realised that the junta leader was me! I sat into the passenger seat and tried to pull the door closed, but it wouldn't budge. 'Sit still,' Jose said to me, and one of my military men came over to heave the door closed with a big thud. It was one of those armoured Mercs, which I found alarming. He then called out to one of his colleagues to mount his motorcycle – or I think he did anyway, because the exchange was in Spanish – and the man got up on his motorbike, and so did another one and then another and another. The Four Horsemen of the Apocalypse accompanied us all the way to San Miguel, along with Jose, who explained that this kind of thing is entirely normal in Mexico, where businessmen are regularly kidnapped for ransom. I was mortified to stick out like that, while my colleagues sailed through Mexico City on their little bus – what a statement!

I loved Mexico, but North America holds a special place in my heart because I go there every year for seven weeks, so the place feels like home to me. I particularly love New York, as it has a great energy to it. I'd say I've been there over fifty times at this stage, but I also like the laid-back cities on North America's north-west coast, like Seattle or Vancouver, in Canada. They feel more 'Irish', if you like: less reserved and more relaxed.

Anyway, one year my sister Susan happened to be visiting New York while I was working there. She was bringing her son, Ian, for a trip and I said, 'We'll do the town.' Now, I'd been given a present of a travel clock from Tiffany & Co., which didn't work. I'd set it for 6.30 a.m. and it'd go off at 9.00 a.m. and so on. When I brought it back to the store, they were very kind and offered me a voucher for the amount plus another $100 as a little gift – now, that's customer service!

After taking Susan and Ian to FAO Schwarz and the other sights, I suggested Tiffany, because of my voucher. Our cousin Ellen, who lives in New York, had recently got engaged and I thought she'd like to have a look at the diamonds, so she came along for the jaunt. When we got there, we were browsing away and one of the assistants happened to notice that we were Irish. 'Oh,' she said, 'Madame Schlumberger owns a castle in Dublin.' Madame Schlumberger was the daughter of the famed Jean Schlumberger, one of Tiffany's iconic designers. She'd married a man called Primat and had ended up owning Luttrellstown Castle. Now, I remembered Madame Primat well because Nuala Roche had sold Reen-na-Furrira, her magnificent house in Sneem, to her. Madame Primat had been looking for a little bolthole (!) in the west of Ireland, and a local estate agent had contacted Nuala. At the time, Nuala had family staying at the house and had to spend a morning stuffing sleeping bags into wardrobes and that kind of thing. She was most reluctant to receive Madame Primat, because she was relaxing at her holiday home, but the woman appeared on her doorstep. Nuala dutifully showed her around, and when she brought Madame into one of the guest rooms she casually mentioned that Charles de Gaulle had stayed there once, whereupon Madame Primat burst into tears! It turned out that the lady was a huge fan of Charles de Gaulle and this little nugget of information sealed the deal.

Anyway, the sales lady was so taken with us she asked us if we'd like to have a look at Jean Schlumberger's famous baguette diamonds – he invented the baguette cut for precious stones. We jumped at the chance and were ushered into a private room upstairs, where a little velvet pouch was produced and there they were! Seeing something that beautiful was a wonderful experience.

One of the things I find a little awkward about the US, though, is the driving. Now, I'm a fairly adventurous driver, probably because I spend such a lot of time in my car, and because I spend so much time in the US, where they are pretty conservative drivers, the local police have had occasion, shall we say, to stop me.

On one occasion, I was leaving New York City with my great friend Jean McCluskey. Now, Jean and I have known each other since 1979, when we met on an Irish Tourist

Board trip to the US, and we've been friends ever since. I always stay with Jean when I'm in New York. The two of us were heading to Albany, in upstate New York, on sales calls for the Irish Tourist Board. The police are very keen on stopping people for speeding on this particular highway, and as we drove along we spotted a few people being pulled over. I decided to be cautious and set the cruise control for 59mph to make sure I didn't break the speed limit. I wasn't a bit worried, apart from the fact that I had to drive at 59mph, which is a killer for me, but that's another story! Anyway, I passed a police car at one stage, but I thought I was fine because I double checked the speedometer to make sure I was only doing 59 mph. I did look in my rear-view mirror and noticed that the police car was pulling out, but I kept going because I hadn't done anything wrong. Then I suddenly noticed that his lights were flashing: 'Oh,' I said to Jean, 'he's putting on his lights.'

'For what?'

'I don't know,' I said, and kept driving for a little bit and then suddenly I realised it was me he was interested in. I pulled in and the police car pulled in behind me. I was careful to stay in the car, with my hands at ten to two, determined not to put a foot wrong. The policeman got out of his car and came up to my window and barked, 'Give me your paperwork.' I explained that Jean was the insured person and I was just driving, whereupon Jean started rummaging through what seemed like 700 sheets of paper, looking for the correct paperwork, while the policeman said to me, 'Step out of the car please.'

Obediently, I got out and followed the policeman back to his car. He got in, and like an eejit I went to open the passenger door and climb in, whereupon he barked at me to stay put. So, yours truly had to bend down and stick my head in the passenger window.

'I'm sorry, officer,' I said. 'I'm not sure why I've been stopped.'

'Take your head out of the car and stand on the kerb,' he yelled. I jumped back on the kerb and waited. It was snowing by this stage, and I wasn't happy, but I kept quiet. Eventually, he said, 'You have committed an offence under section three subsection four of the blah, blah...' I can't remember what he said exactly because I had no clue what he was talking about, but then he said, 'Did you not see my clapperboard arrow?'

I thought I'd misheard him. 'I beg your pardon?'

'Did you not see my clapperboard arrow?' he repeated, pointing towards the rear of the car.

I looked down the road, as if something might be visible there. 'I'm awfully sorry, officer, I can't see anything.'

He sighed. 'One minute,' he said and he began hunting on his onboard computer for the offence of which I was guilty. 'I have to phone the depot,' he said eventually. 'Madge, Code number 57/d/e....' He began mumbling a lot of jargon into his walkie-talkie.

'I'm sorry, officer,' I persisted. 'I still don't know why you stopped me.'

'Please look at the clapperboard arrow,' he barked again, and I gingerly put my head in the passenger window to see what he was talking about. He flicked a button on the dashboard and on the rear window shelf, lo and behold, a mechanical arrow appeared. Now, you would want to have bionic vision to see this arrow! The way it works is that if the arrow points out, you are not allowed, by law, to pass a stopped police car on the inside lane. You should pass on the very outside lane if this is the case. The reason for this is so that you don't accidentally hit a policeman or a person who the policeman has stopped. I can see the logic, but as I stood there covered in snow, I thought, For God's sake.

After bowing and scraping, I was allowed to drive off again, chastened, but to this day, when I watch my favourite TV show in America, *Cops*, I cheer when someone drives into the back of a police car! I shouldn't, I know, but I do. But it doesn't end there: I was to face a fine of $180 for this infraction. So I wrote to the presiding judge in the case, who had an Irish name, and explained the unfairness, as I saw it, of the charge. The judge replied that he'd be delighted to hear me, but I'd have to appear in person. As I'd gone home to Kenmare at this stage, I couldn't help thinking it would be a very expensive hearing!

Now, I have to admit that that isn't the only time I've had a brush with the law because of my driving. In fact – and you'll have to forgive this little digression from my American tales – I did come a cropper in Monasterevin, Co. Kildare once, on my way to the Eurovision Song Contest, which was being held in Dublin that year.

Maura Lee, the producer of the show, had asked me to go, and I was delighted with myself. I decided to drive up from Kenmare on the day and drop in to see my old friend Jean – the same Jean with whom I'd travelled to Albany. Jean had had a baby the night before in the National Maternity Hospital, and she was by herself as her husband was in New York. As usual I was miles behind time, so I was flying into Monasterevin. Now, there's a long stretch of road at one point, and I was stuck behind three cars that were going very slowly and I was getting bit impatient. So I indicated and pulled out to overtake all three cars, passing the first car and then the second ... and then I realised the third car was a garda car. I did everything right, I told myself, as I passed him, indicated and then pulled in in front of him, booting it along, of course. Like an eejit, I thought I'd gotten away with it, but the next minute I saw the blue light flashing in my rear-view mirror.

I pulled over and waited, and, sure enough, my friendly garda got out of the car and came towards me – he was so friendly, in fact, that he opened the passenger door and sat in beside me. I couldn't help thinking of the contrast with my experience in Albany.

'You're biting the bullet a bit,' said he.

'I am,' I agreed. 'I'm going to Dublin to see a friend who's just had a baby.' (I didn't mention that I was also going to the Eurovision after). 'Her husband's in New York and I want to give her moral support,' I explained.

'Well, if you keep driving at the speed you're going, you won't see any babies.'

'No, officer,' I agreed, and I took the lecture that followed. Then I zoomed off to Dublin to see Jean and go to the Eurovision. Now, I didn't think he was going to summons me, but three months later I was duly summonsed to appear in court, along with half the country, it seemed. It all moved very fast, with each case being processed at the speed of light. And then my case was called, 'Francis Brennan versus the State.'

My friendly garda took the stand. 'On the day appointed, Mr Brennan was driving at 89 miles an hour on the approach to Monasterevin and passed out three cars.'

'Had he any comment when stopped? ' the judge asked.

'Oh, yes, his wife had a baby that day in Dublin and he was driving up to visit her.'

From the bowels of the packed courtroom, I jumped up. 'Excuse me,' I interrupted. 'Can I just say that I'm not married and I don't have any children. I was going to see a friend of mine who was home from New York to give her support.'

'Oh,' the judge said. 'And where do you live?'

'I'm the owner of the Park Hotel in Kenmare, Your Lordship,' I replied.

'And did you come up all this way?' The judge looked impressed. Thank God, I thought, it's going to be all right.

But then my friendly garda intervened. 'Did you not see me, when you were overtaking all of those cars?'

'Well, if I'd seen you, I wouldn't have been speeding.'

I got the Probation Act, and it was on to the next case!

But I digress, even though I think this story nicely illustrates the difference between Irish and American approaches to law enforcement.

I think my favourite American story is about the time I impersonated the Irish Ambassador to the US at the St Patrick's Day parade in Kentucky – as you do!

In 1983, the Irish Tourist Board brought a group of people from Ireland to the US to promote Ireland; people like Maureen Potter, John B. Keane and Bryan McMahon were flown over to do radio and TV interviews during St Patrick's week. It was a big success and Ireland Inc got a lot of excellent PR from the visit. The following year, there was no budget to do a similar event, but the Americans were still looking for Irish people because the promotion had been such a success the year before.

Now, in Lexington, the Irish Bluegrass Society, no less, were looking for an Irishman to come and be grand marshal of the Lexington St Patrick's Day parade, and Simon O'Hanlon, the Irish Tourist Board's PR man at the time, hit on little old me. I'd been doing my usual sales tour of the country, so I was ideally placed, even if I had no idea what would be involved. What does a grand marshal do anyway? I thought. But I wasn't too worried, because I expected that, like all the people who'd been out the year before, I'd have media training beforehand.

Off I went on my sales tour, travelling for two weeks, from San Francisco to New York and all over the country. I kept thinking that at some stage I'd be taken aside and tutored. Not at all. On the Thursday before St Patrick's Day, an envelope appeared on the desk in my hotel room. 'Enjoy Lexington,' was scribbled on the front. Inside was a plane ticket.

I rang Simon in a panic. 'What am I going to do and who am I going to meet and what am I going to say?'

'Ah, go on, you'll be grand,' was Simon's helpful response.

I'd arranged a weekend in Boston, but I had to cancel and head off to Lexington into the unknown – I didn't even know where it was!

Things didn't start well when I missed my flight, because of a fire at Logan Airport in Boston, and then had to make a connection at La Guardia for Lexington. I was running hours late and I was in a bit of a state. I had a ton of baggage: a big hard shell suitcase, a few suit carriers and other bags, which I had to drag along behind me as I charged down to the gate. I arrived out of breath to be told that the flight had closed.

'Oh, you can't do that,' I said. 'I'm grand marshal of the St Patrick's Day parade tomorrow in Kentucky and I can't let them down.'

'I'm sorry,' the lady at the gate said. 'Once a flight is closed, it never reopens.'

I insisted, 'Please call down to the pilot and get me on, because I have to go.'

She phoned the plane and after a quick exchange she ushered me down the gangway. I shot on board and the plane immediately started moving, and there I was with all my goods and chattels.

'Give me that suitcase,' the air stewardess said crossly. 'And take a seat because we're moving.' I walked down the aisle and was a bit surprised to find that all the other passengers were African American and about 7 foot tall. It turned out that I'd caught a flight with the Harlem Globetrotters! They too were going to the parade to take part, and I was delighted to tell the giant of a man sitting next to me that I was to be grand marshal. Not that I had a clue who the Harlem Globetrotters were.

The plane arrived in Lexington and off I got with my two-ton suitcase and my carrier. I saw a red carpet and a brass band and a big crowd of people gathered, clapping and cheering. 'Isn't that nice,' I said to myself. 'The Harlem Globetrotters will be pleased.' After pulling the wheels of my case across the red carpet, I clattered into the airport in search of my contact, a Mr Enright. Everybody in arrivals was looking out of the window, delighted at the spectacle, and nobody seemed to be waiting for me, so I went over and sat down and watched the comings and goings.

'What's all the excitement?' I asked the girl sitting beside me, who was waiting for her family.

'Oh that's for the Irish Ambassador. He's coming to lead the parade.'

The penny dropped. It was all for me – and here I was, sitting inside the terminal. I thought I was going to die! Quite honestly, I still get butterflies at the thought of it. It turned out that Governor Brown of Kentucky, the entire

Irish Bluegrass Society, a band playing an Irish tune that I'd failed to notice and everyone who was anyone was on the carpet – and I'd walked right by them all.

I located a nice girl who'd been greeting the passengers and I explained that I was the man they were all waiting for.

'Oh, we'll have to get you back out,' she said. 'Give me all of those things and you walk out and come back in again.'

So, off I went. I walked out to this line of officials and I came up behind them. 'Excuse me. I think you're looking for me.'

One of them turned around. 'No, we're waiting for Francis Brennan, the Irish Ambassador.'

'Well, that's me.' May God strike me down at the lie, I thought – but I could hardly tell them otherwise.

'We thought you'd be an old fellow,' he said, looking at me doubtfully.

'No, we have young people in Ireland as well,' I said.

We decided I would have to do it all again, so off I went around to the back of the plane, up the stairs, into the plane, and then out again, like Ronald Reagan, and down the steps to shake the Governor's hand.

'I'm delighted to be here on behalf of the Irish government to lead the parade,' I said. I felt I had no choice but to continue the ruse. And on the local TV news that night, I have to say I looked the business!

The Governor had provided a big car for me and two policemen were with me the whole time. In my capacity as Ambassador, I was provided with a beautiful suite in a hotel and a lovely dinner, and the next morning I had breakfast with the Governor in the mansion. I was in too deep now!

For the parade itself, I was to sit in his car waving to everybody, which was grand, and then it occurred to me, 'Oh my God, I have nothing green.' What Ambassador doesn't have a green tie on St Patrick's Day? Off I went into some mall in search of a green tie, and succeeded in buying a ferociously expensive tie in roaring green (I only ever wore it once). And when I came out of the shop, could I find my way back? I was completely lost and had no idea how I'd explain this to the Governor. After a few minutes' panic, I found my way back and made my appearance as grand marshal at the parade. I was a huge success and had the most marvellous time.

The next day, I was brought to a horse farm that an Irishman, Michael Osborne, a member of the Bluegrass Society and the previous grand marshal, was running for a Minneapolis businessman, and I nodded along as they all talked about colts and fillies and the like – sure, what would I know? I only know they have four legs and a tail! I didn't appreciate that I was visiting Calumet Farm, only one of the biggest names in American horse racing. Anyway, I got away with it, and off I went to the horse racing the following day, where I was bestowed with the distinction of being an honorary Kentucky Colonel, which grants lots of privileges for the Kentucky Derby – so I'd be front row!

I carried off my duties as the fake Ambassador with style, I like to think, but when I got back to New York I caught Simon by the throat. However, he was completely unrepentant. 'Sure, we knew you'd be grand and we've had fantastic news back about how you've been such a success.' And I only one step ahead of the firing squad!

Looking back over my diaries, I'm almost surprised at just how much I've travelled in the past number of years. Sometimes it all seems to merge into a blur of airports, cars and taxis, so it's been such a pleasure to remember some of the highlights. Nowadays, when we're all bombarded with images of famous places on the Internet, it feels like a privilege to have visited some of these places in person, a privilege that not everyone can share. But I think the key is to be open-minded, whether at home or abroad, and also to make the most of the encounters and the chats you have with people along the way. That way, you make the most of life and connect with other people, and that's what it's all about. Happiness doesn't depend on having visited the Empire State Building or Sydney Opera House, but it does depend on making connections with other people and appreciating every moment, and that's what travel has given me, along with an appreciation for my friends, with whom I've been lucky enough to share so many journeys.

I can fully appreciate that travel isn't affordable for everyone, particularly if you have a family and other priorities are in play, but curiosity is, I think, one of the great positives in life. Even if you never travel beyond your front gate, having a curious mind will keep you young and interested in the world. I think the important thing is not to be close-minded, but to continue to be flexible and open throughout life, whether you've been to Acapulco or just to Athlone for the weekend. Life is fleeting, so I try to make the very most of it. I can hear you say, 'That's all very well for you, Francis. You don't have a family/dog/granny that needs minding.' That's true, but I have other responsibilities so I try to make time for what matters to me in life: my family, my work, my friends, my faith. And these are the things that will continue to matter, whether or not I ever get on an aeroplane again. After all, it's not the destination, but the journey, that counts.

———

Have you set yourself any goals recently? I don't mean to climb Everest next December or to invent the next big thing in technology. I mean small, achievable goals that will build to bigger ones. If you want to travel around Spain, perhaps start by taking a Spanish class; or if you want to play golf, maybe start with an outing to the local pitch and putt course. The important thing is not to be unrealistic and then get disappointed with yourself.
Start small and build from there.

7.

*A Hug
Goes a Long Way*

'God has no religion.'

Mahatma Gandhi

When I was discussing the content of this book with my publishers, they were very keen for me to include a chapter on my spirituality, because they felt that it would be of interest and help to readers. Now, while I am indeed a man of faith, I consider my religion to be a very personal thing, and I have no intention of converting anyone or being seen as a holy Joe. It's something that's guided me throughout my life, but it's a private thing and when I speak about it I feel a bit self-conscious. I don't think that 'religion' or 'faith' is any one fixed thing, but is really a way of looking at the world and seeing something more in it; something that can't be explained, but that makes you look at things in a different way and connect with others in a different way. I believe that's what faith is: what you bring to every encounter with another person.

'What you are is God's gift to you; what you become is your gift to God.' The man who said this was a Swiss theologian called Hans Urs von Balthasar. You may not have heard of him – I certainly hadn't before writing this book – but I think that what he says here sums up my own beliefs beautifully. We are all on a path through life and we begin with what we've been given, and, as we go on, we hope that we can 'give back' by being the very best person that we can be, and by giving to others without waiting for them to be grateful. If we call that 'God', that's fine, because I firmly believe that God is in everyone and everything. It's not about priests or nuns or mass – even though I go to mass myself – it's about life itself.

But I'll begin with a priest story, just for the fun of it. It was 1986 or 1987 and I was staying in Loews Regency Hotel in New York on my annual business trip when I bumped into John Fitzpatrick, of the hotel family, who was visiting the city for the first time. He needed to go to the bank and, because I was headed downtown towards the Irish Tourist offices, I said I'd bring him with me. Since it was only 8.40 a.m., it occurred to me that the bank wouldn't be open yet, so I said, 'Come on and we'll have a bit of breakfast.' We went into a typical New York diner, in a basement – we were sitting in hell, basically – and we took a seat at the counter.

Now, the waitress was about seventy, and I couldn't help thinking that if she was my mother I couldn't bear her working at that age, but Mrs Overall herself seemed to be doing just fine. This was before Starbuck's, soy lattes and that kind of thing, and they just had one of those old-fashioned coffee machines behind the counter. I recognised it, because we'd bought one for the Park Hotel Kenmare. It was called a Bunn-o-Matic, and the reason we'd bought it was because MacDonald's had one and I'd thought that if they had it, it must work. But there was one fault with it: after a while the teat that hung down into the pot would stretch and it'd start dripping. It was easy enough to fix it – you just turned the teat upside down and hey presto.

I said to Mrs Overall, 'I like your coffee machine.'

'Oh, it's driving me mad,' she said, 'because it keeps dripping.'

I replied, 'I can fix that if you let me in behind the counter.' In I hopped, turned the teat around, screwed it back on and, lo and behold, no drips. She was delighted and we started chatting. Were we from Ireland, she wondered.

We were, we told her, whereupon she revealed that she'd been born in Ireland but had actually been raised in

Scotland, because her parents, who were potato pickers from Donegal, had gone there to work. And, once they'd raised the fare, they came to the US and had never returned. It was the story of so many Irish emigrants, and we chatted away about the US and about what things were like in the old country. I really felt for this lady, because here she was, still working away in her old age.

And then she said, eyeing our suits and ties, 'Can I ask you a personal question? What are ye?'

'What do you mean?' I said.

'Well, you know about the coffee machine and about Ireland, so what are ye?'

'Well, have a guess,' I said, laughing.

'Well, ye wouldn't be two priests, would ye?'

John and I were tickled pink!

If you asked me where my faith came from, I wouldn't really be able to put my finger on it. Like most Irish people growing up in the 1950s and 1960s, we were Catholics, but I can't say that my parents or brothers and sisters were wildly religious. I think I was always the religious one and maybe this might have had something to do with the amount of time I spent in hospital as a child. I remember lying in the Mater Hospital after one operation, and being in a lot of pain, but I didn't want to disturb the nurses and so I just focused on the light coming from the ceiling to distract myself. As a child, I used to imagine that the light was coming from heaven and I'd pray to God to make the pain go away. It always did, and I suppose I began to believe that my prayers would be answered. Growing up, to me God wasn't to be feared, in spite of the Christian Brothers' best efforts, but I saw him as a protector; as a presence in my life when I most needed it.

I also feel that my faith gave me a structure when I needed it. I have a clear memory of my Confirmation, which I attended in my blazer, cap and short trousers, a rosette in my lapel with a miraculous medal on it. Off I went, by myself, as I recall, to the big church in Westland Row. I distinctly remember that the bishop asked me a question and I was delighted to be able to answer it. Do you remember that – the fear when he'd be coming towards you with his staff and his pointy hat? I passed the test with flying colours. I took the pledge not to drink alcohol, and I've never broken it. In fact, I've never felt the desire to.

I suppose I did follow the rules in the 'difficult' teenage years, with the sex and the drugs and that kind of thing, and then by the time I got to my middle twenties, after keeping the rules for so long, I couldn't work out why I'd be breaking them. And I never felt any desire to because they'd served me very well. I suppose part of this was because I was working during all of those rebellious years, and I was absolutely not a rebel, even though I was good fun. Susan and Kate were out morning, noon and night, and if it wasn't a Ferrari turning up at the door, it was a Lamborghini, and if it wasn't a Lamborghini, it was a Bentley!

Part of the reason I didn't rebel, I think, was because I always had the responsibility at home when Dad was sick and when things were tight. I didn't even think about it: I just put money on the table every Friday. And I suppose when you get older you realise that that was kind of important. It grows on you and you don't think about it, and all of a sudden there's a hotel and seventy people behind you, and you think, 'Oh, better just get on with it, Francis.' I've had responsibility all my life. Even when I go on holiday, I'm responsible. I buy the tickets and people ask me where we'll go for lunch – I take it on, I suppose. And perhaps my faith, and following its rules, is an outlet for me. It's good to know that someone else is responsible for me and that I have that safety net in times of difficulty. Mind you, I have promised myself that the day I retire I don't want to have grass to cut or leaves to tidy – I want nothing. If I won the Lotto in the morning, what difference would it make? Someone would still have to run the hotel!

So, I've signed up for my faith, and I've always believed that if you enlist you have to soldier, which either makes me a great fellow or an eejit! But as a member of the Catholic Church, I believe that I have to follow its rules. My faith gives me a set of rules or guidelines to live by, which give my life meaning. I read an interview with Woody Allen, the film director, recently, because his movie, *Irrational Man*, deals with matters of faith. In it, he said, 'It makes life better when there's something to believe in.' I firmly believe this and couldn't imagine what my life would be like if I didn't have that something. Life has to have meaning, I think, whether that's through faith or family or simply a belief in other people – it doesn't matter. But I can't imagine what life would be like without meaning. How would I make sense of it all? So many things are sent to test us nowadays and so many bad things go on in the world that it's hard to imagine how we'd manage without believing that there's enough good in people to counteract that.

I think we've lost sight of that belief a bit in Ireland in recent years. Not just because of the Celtic Tiger, although that did have a part to play, but because we've forgotten the role faith has to play in life – and not just the Catholic faith, but a faith that makes you believe in something higher than yourself. I think that other countries and societies have a lot to teach us in this way.

I remember once going to a Confirmation ceremony in St Miguel de Allende – home of the firework Jesus! As a regular mass-goer, I am given 'time out' to go to mass on a Sunday during conferences. Seeking out a suitable time and place, I checked out the local church in San Miguel and the notice-board on the front door seemed to say that mass was at 9.30 a.m. Grand, I thought, and I ducked out of the meeting at 9.20 a.m. to head off to mass. When I got near the church I noticed a few youngsters dressed in white and I thought, Oh, that's nice, they must dress up for the feast day.

When I went into the church, I found it completely empty, which I thought was a bit odd as mass was due to start any minute. But I took up my seat on the right-hand side of the church and waited patiently. The appointed time arrived, but no action. And then, at 9.40 a.m., a huge crowd arrived, all children, and all dressed in white. Well, a kind of off-white in some cases. The children appeared to range in age from ten to fifteen, boys and girls, and they all sat very reverently in the pews. Suddenly, I noticed that I was the only adult in this sea of white-clad children and I thought, I'd better get out of here and leave them be, so I moved to a pew in the side aisles, which duly began to fill up. By 9.50 a.m., the church was packed and I'd moved to a vantage point on a side altar, where I could see the whole church. I'd say there were close to a thousand children in the church, in their off-white splendour. Some of the outfits, I noticed, had clearly been passed down in the family, as the trousers had a series of horizontal lines at the ankles where they'd been 'upped' or 'downed' according to need. The girls looked angelic in their veils – many of them yellowed with age – but they still looked so reverent on this their Communion or Confirmation day (I didn't know which).

I happened to notice people scurrying around with paperwork, looking anxious; it was clear that these were birth or baptismal certs that had to be in order for a child to proceed. Some weren't in order, it seemed, and it was hard to watch as a teacher remonstrated with parents whose paperwork wasn't complete. These were country people, some of whom would have had limited literacy skills. I also noticed a flashbulb going off every now and again, and then a photographer appeared, photographing each child individually on a very cleverly reconfigured Polaroid camera that allowed him to take nine shots to every regular Polaroid print. What he'd done was force a piece of aluminium in front of the lens so that a postage-stamp-sized shot of each child would appear on the print. He'd cut this shot out and push it into a clear key fob and then hand it to each child. I wondered if some of these children were seeing themselves in a photograph for the first time. The photographer then sought the princely sum of 50 cents for each photo/fob. If parents didn't have the money, he took the key fob back.

It took me a while to fully understand this *modus operandi* and, suffice to say, I left the church a few hundred dollars lighter because I didn't want any child to go without a memento of their precious day. I say this not to let you all know what a great man I am, but to say that I was so impressed by the simple faith of these children that I felt they should have something to remember the day by.

On leaving the church, I passed a small side altar and was astonished to find a statue of someone very familiar. He was standing, staff in hand, on a globe, around which wound a number of snakes. It was none other than St Patrick, banishing the snakes from Ireland. I clearly wasn't the first Irishman to attend services in St Miguel, but I have never been able to find out how on earth the statue came to be there. Maybe I'd been enticed into this particular church on this special day for the children of San Miguel de Allende.

I suppose it's tempting enough to praise more traditional societies for hanging on to their faith, but I think they have something to teach us about what is important: even though they have nothing in material terms, they have everything spiritually. I also feel that a country's spirit is very much in its faith – look at Nepal and what a spiritual place that is, and how that is reflected in the Dalai Lama, a man I admire enormously; or look at Spain. Once, we had a Small Luxury Hotels of the World conference in Arcos de la Frontera, which is in the Jerez region of the south of Spain, where they make the sherry. The daughter of the house was called Rocio Domecq; she was a salesgirl for SLHW, and her brother was one of the biggest bullfighters at the time! I went to a bull-fight at their invitation, which wasn't an experience I'd care to repeat. Mind you, they gave me the bull's ear as a souvenir, which is a great honour! Anyway, because of the bullfight, mass wasn't until nine o'clock at night. We were starving because we hadn't had dinner yet, but we had to sit on the wall outside the church after mass waiting for Rocio, who was still inside praying to her name saint – you are given a saint in your local church and you have that saint for life. We didn't go to dinner until 10.40 p.m., but I admired Rocio and her family very much for their honest-to-God approach and for their strong beliefs.

Of course, like everyone else's, my faith is tested. I remember that my brother John was in the process of buying Dromquinna Manor, where he now has his wedding business, when he went into hospital for an operation on his gall bladder. It turned out he had stage four non-Hodgkin lymphoma, which, you can imagine, was a terrible blow. I said a prayer for him every day because that was my way of dealing with what had happened. I'm sure that everyone has his or her own way, but I found my faith a great comfort to me. The Lord moves in mysterious ways, and John recovered, but, as you may know, the disease never goes away; it just lies dormant. I really admire John's fortitude in dealing with his illness, but I know that, for me, my faith sustains me in times like this, even though it can be difficult to understand why these things happen. I know that many people think there is no explanation, that life is just a series of random coincidences, but for me it's important to make sense of these and to know that there is somewhere I can go to do so.

When I think of my faith being tested, one memory in particular comes to mind. My first trip to Lourdes was thirty-two years ago, and I've been going ever since, from 2 to 7 September every year. I go with Kerry Diocesan Pilgrimage, with about six hundred people, fifty of whom are patients in hospitals all over the county. The patients stay in the hospital in Lourdes and my job, along with a lovely lady called Angie, is to look after specialist food for those who need it, for example those who are coeliacs, potassium intolerant, gluten intolerant and that kind of thing. Angie and I organise our menus in July and oversee them when we are there. It's a demanding schedule: we go to the hospital at 7.00 a.m. and don't finish until 11.00 p.m., but we just get on with it – it's only for five days after all, and the people we are looking after deserve it.

Now, my first year in Lourdes, I went to the baths to help out. Every year, an unbelievable 350,000 people use the baths in Lourdes, and I volunteered to help some of the disabled people into and out of the baths, which are filled with Lourdes water. The water is holy, because Holy Mary told St Bernadette, 'Go drink at the spring and wash yourself there.' And that's what people do: they come into the baths to be fully immersed, head and all, in Lourdes water with the hope of being cured of whatever illness they have. It's very cold and the whole process lasts about a minute. So far, there have been sixty-nine official miracles at Lourdes, where people have emerged illness-free from their stay there: either the mind is a remarkable thing, or miracles do actually happen!

Now, on the day that I was there helping out at the baths, this German man came in with his son, who was severely physically handicapped. The son was about thirty-five, and the poor man was bewildered and confused, but we eventually managed to get him down the steps and into the bath. His poor father was up at the top of the steps, and he gave this wail of distress. He began to cry at the state of his poor son. 'What is going to happen to my son when I die?' he kept saying.

I thought, He needs a hug, that man. But the 'machine' doesn't allow for that kind of thing; there's no time for compassion because there are hundreds of people waiting their turn. That poor father hoped for a miracle, which never came. Who knows why that man wasn't cured and others were? To me, that is the mystery; you have to keep believing even when it's hard.

I have thought about that poor disabled man a thousand times since, but I've had to accept that God didn't see fit to cure him, for whatever reason. And I think about his father, and it reminds me that we do not know what the stranger we pass on the street is dealing with in his or her life. That morning in the baths affected me for ever. I wasn't able to go back to the baths ever again. The experience was too emotional and even now, thirty-two years later, I can see that man and his father still.

I suppose that my experience in Lourdes could have put me off God or lessened my faith in him, but it didn't. I'm guided by the Lord in everything, which may sound a bit 'holy' to you, but it's true. I consider my faith a blessing and am happy to work within the confines of my faith. And it's served me well, as a moral code. I've never shot anyone, stolen money or committed any other big sin! I'm fully aware that non-religious people and people of other religions have their own moral codes, and I don't consider mine to be any better than theirs, but it works for me.

I think that my faith can also make me a role model for younger people and I try to put as much as I can into that role. I'm not suggesting for a minute that I know better than anyone else, but it's something that I enjoy and that inspires me. I work with lots of young people at the Park Hotel Kenmare, and, on the day of induction for new staff, I always give them the mass times in Kenmare – Saturday at 8.00 p.m.; Sunday at 9.30 a.m. and noon – and I always say, 'Don't lose your religion because you work in the hotel business.' That's easy to do, of course, because mass times clash with the busiest times of service at the hotel; for example, the breakfast rush is at 9.30 a.m. – or it is in Ireland! And I always check up on staff I know are interested in going to mass. Say there's a nice country girl who I know would normally go to mass, I might wait a week or two and then say,

'Have you been to mass?' And if she says, 'No,' I don't push it. I just ask the once! But I think mass gives young people something to hold on to in life.

As for me, I never miss mass – it's not that I'm a holy Joe; it's just a nice habit and it helps me to remember what's important in life. I remember when I worked in the Sligo Park Hotel it was a bit difficult, because I'd always be on for breakfast in the morning and then again in the evening, and it'd be go, go, go all day. But I knew there was a 6.30 a.m. mass down town, and so I bought a bike so that I could zip down and then be back for breakfast. I've been to mass all over the world, and I like it because the sense of community is so good and because it helps me to remember that we're all the same. When I'm in San Francisco, I always go to the church in Chinatown, and frequently I am invited back to someone's house for their post-mass coffee morning. And of course, the Irish are always a big hit, with our stories.

In all the time I've been at the Park Hotel Kenmare, only five people have asked for time off on a Sunday morning, but I'm happy to give it. I remember one was a lovely Hungarian lad, who not only wanted time off on a Sunday morning, but insisted on not eating breakfast.

I was mystified. 'Would you not eat your breakfast?'

'Oh, I have to fast from the night before for mass,' he told me.

'Good Lord,' says I. 'It's only one hour in Ireland!'

I have an immediate affinity with young people, because a proportion of my staff are young, so I try to help them where I can. I think that sometimes a chat with a more mature person when you're young can really inspire you. I can think of situations where this has happened, where I've seen that spark in some young person and I can tell they have that special quality. Also, every year I go to colleges – Cathal Brugha Street and Shannon College of Hotel Management – and speak to a hundred or so students. I tell my story and I can see young people thinking, I could do that. It might lift five people out of a hundred, and isn't that great? My mum has that ability too, because she's able to help people to relax and she's a great listener.

Over the years in the hotel, I've had situations where young people were in difficulty and I've tried to help as best I can. And it's not because I feel that I have some divine mission, but because I remember times when I was young when a chat with an older colleague really helped. I remember, one year, money went missing from the staff hall at the hotel. Now, there was a big inquisition, and we narrowed it down to a few people who were in the area at the time. I brought this one particular boy into the office and we chatted away. I made no accusations, just talked around the subject for a bit until I felt he was relaxed, and then I brought up the issue. Did he have any clue as to who might have taken the money? And then he burst into tears. It turned out he was a kleptomaniac, a genuine one, who had had the condition since he was a child. Every time he'd go to a birthday party he'd have to bring something home – a Matchbox car or some other toy – and then when he'd get home he'd wonder why he'd taken it. Wherever he went, he had to take something and he just couldn't control the impulse. He was in an awful state. 'I'm not like that, Mr Brennan,' he said. 'It's not me, but I just do it.'

The minute he said that, I knew he had a problem. I had a great friend in Cork who was a psychologist, so I rang him and said, 'Look, I want you to do me a favour. I have a young fellow here who needs your help.' And the good doctor sorted him out. I'm still in touch with this man today and he's never looked back.

I'm not telling you this story so that you can admire me; I'm simply telling you because I really do believe in the power of making a difference to others, and that's central to my beliefs. I think every one of us has it within us to connect with other human beings and to help them where we possibly can. Anyone can do it. I was at a hotel conference in the Algarve not so long ago, and I was sitting by the pool one morning when I saw this poor man in floods of tears on a lounger. The pool attendant came up and sat beside him and proceeded to rub his back. I couldn't help thinking that that was a bit forward – we don't offer that kind of service at the Park Hotel Kenmare! The next morning at breakfast, I saw the poor man again. One of the staff was chatting quietly to him, clearly sympathising with him. When I asked the receptionist about him later, she told me that he was a regular guest who came to stay four or five times a year, and he'd just learned of a family crisis. Because the staff knew him so well, they thought nothing of comforting him. A hug clearly meant a lot to this young man.

Recently, I bumped into a friend, Donal, in New York and he told me his very own kindness story, which amused me no end. I'd been telling him about meeting my 'street bum' friend in Pittsburgh, who I told you about in the Introduction to this book. Donal has been living in the US for years, working in construction. Now, some years ago, on Christmas Day, the only day that the sites close, and he was alone in his apartment, poor man, far away from his family in Ireland, and he thought, I'd better go out and get a bit of dinner. So, off he went to one of the restaurants that was open on Christmas Day – it *is* New York! – and ordered a turkey dinner to go. As he walked down the street with his turkey dinner, he spied a street bum and he thought, Well, as bad and all as I am, he's worse off. He thought that maybe he could help him, so he headed back to the restaurant to order another turkey dinner for the man. And then he thought, Sure, it's Christmas. So he went into a shop and bought a six-pack of beer and twenty cigarettes – well, what harm could it do on Christmas Day?

Delighted with himself, Donal walked back down the street and said to the man, 'Happy Christmas. I got you a little something.'

'Oh,' the man said, emerging from his huddle. 'You're very good.'

Donal handed over the turkey dinner and told the man to enjoy it, and then he said, 'Don't tell anyone, but I have a treat for you.' And he handed the man the six-pack and the cigarettes. The man fell upon them, and then he looked at the turkey dinner and said to Donal, 'Oh, you can hold onto that, I'm not hungry.'

And the moral of the story is … sometimes people just don't want to be helped!

Joking apart, I think that a lot of the time people are glad to make that connection with another human being, like my friend in Pittsburgh. It made a big difference to both of us, I think. It made me realise what a fortunate soul I am and how blessed I've been in life, not just with what I've been given, but with my positive outlook and my determination to keep on going, no matter what. I also know that my faith makes me happy, because it gives my life meaning. Do you know that there are sixty billionaires living in New York between

Fifty-Ninth and Eightieth Street? And I bet not all of them are happy. Money doesn't make you happy. I know that better than many, I suppose, because I had money and now I don't, relatively speaking. I know that money makes life so much easier, but it doesn't make you content.

I know that the sources of my happiness are things other than money: friends, family, work and the things I enjoy in life – the garden, meeting people, going to interesting places, and doing what I can to make other people happy. And it comes from believing in other people and in something beyond myself. I understand that you don't need religion to be kind to others – but I do think it can enhance you spiritually. And I can tell you with great certainty that doing something good for another person is the easiest way to make yourself happy. Try it!

My faith provides me with so much in life – community, structure, a map to follow – and I don't know where I'd be without it, even though I understand why it might not be as important to others. I can see why people might consider some of the Church's rulings as out of date or old-fashioned, but like any organisation it will have rules we like and rules we don't like. And I prefer to focus my attention on what my faith helps me to do – to be interested in other people and to want to help them, to share with others and to find inner happiness and peace. Who knows where we're all headed when life is over, but to me that isn't the point. I'm not just behaving nicely because I want to get into heaven; I think that what you do in life matters in its own right, and that every moment, every action counts.

———

What do you believe in? It doesn't have to be God; it can be a belief in the goodness of others or in your own abilities, or in justice and fairness. The important thing is to believe in something, because having that belief will give you the power to do great things.

8.
A Few of My Favourite Things

'The most wasted of all days is one without laughter.'
Nicolas Chamfort

And now the end is near, and you know all there is to know about me! Well, nearly all. It's been a great journey for me, thinking and writing about all the steps of my life so far and what's guided me along and made me truly happy. As I said at the beginning of this book, life isn't just fun, and happiness isn't a matter of pretending everything is just perfect – we all have our difficulties and struggles, and we understand that they are part of the fabric of life. What would it be like if it was all a picnic? I think that our struggles and our challenges are what make us who we are. I wouldn't be who I am if it weren't for my foot or all the years of hard work. I also wouldn't be who I am without the support and encouragement of my family, my beliefs or my love of getting out there and meeting the world. This is who I am.

I'm a great believer in living in the moment and in filling your day with the things that bring happiness, and so, in this chapter, I've compiled a little list of the things that are special to me – I'm counting my blessings! Without getting too 'Julie Andrews' about it, here are a few of my favourite things (and people!).

– Humour –

I couldn't get through my day without a laugh or a funny story; humour is something that sustains me and helps me to take life less seriously. I take myself and my work seriously and strive to do my best, but life itself, well, where would we be without a laugh?

− A nice cup of tea −

Milk first, no sugar. The water has to be freshly boiled and made with tea leaves, not bags. Perfect. I'm not difficult to please!

− My friends −

I count myself hugely lucky in this respect. I think that when you are single, like me, and you work all God's hours – like me! – you could end up without friends, but I feel truly blessed that that's not the case. I've been thinking about what friendship means to me, and my definition of a friend is someone you can ring up and say you're coming to stay and they don't do the high dusting. What I mean by this is that friends don't stand on ceremony; you can truly relax and be yourself with your friends, and I really value this.

I met Tony Malone, Martin McNally and Frank Dowling at school in CUS and we are still friends today. I met Jean McCluskey, my friend in New York with whom I stay every single year, through the Irish Tourist Board, as I did Frances and Brian Kennedy, who are lifelong friends. Frances is from Crusheen, Co. Clare, but she and Brian now live in Boston with their three lovely daughters. They used to love when I came to visit, because I always had stories and presents.

The funny thing is I wouldn't say that I'm a brilliant friend, in the sense that I'm never available for a dinner party or that kind of thing. I suppose I'm not someone you can ring to ask to come over and mow the lawn or help you tidy the tool shed! The hotel dominates my life because the hours are so long and I'm so rarely at home, but when I do meet my friends it's just as if I met them yesterday. We take up where we left off. And because I'm away such a lot, I try to keep in touch by phone or send letters or gifts to show my friends that I'm thinking of them. As a single person, the Skål club has allowed me to enjoy my passion for travel. With my little gang of friends, I've done thirty-four trips in total, and I know that I probably wouldn't have gone on as many adventures were it not for them. And the nice thing is that, even as husbands and wives have passed on, the widowed partner continues to travel with us, because we are so close at this stage.

– My mother –

My mother is still alive and still giving out to us. She's a life force and life simply wouldn't be the same without her. And she keeps a close eye on our goings-on. Recently, when I was in the US, she rang to tell me that John had gone on holiday to Spain.

'That's not right,' she protested. 'The two of you out of the country at the same time.'

'But the hotel's closed, Mum,' I said. 'And John Moriarty can easily manage if anything happens.'

'If there was a flood or a fire, there'd be no Brennan there,' she told me. And she's right – she was simply reminding me of my responsibilities! And that's what mothers are for, I think, to make sure that we do our best, even at the age of sixty-two. Mum is also the glue that holds us all together as siblings and we all look to her as the head of the family.

– My home –

Home for me has a great significance. I began, as you know, in my childhood home in Balally, which was originally in an estate of just thirty-seven houses that had been built in 1950. When Mum and Dad moved in in 1951, they had nothing only the house itself. They had Jaffa orange boxes for chairs and a table and that was all – not one other stick of furniture – and they did up one room at a time, as they could afford it. We had a very nice little community, and then in the mid-1960s a developer called Gallagher built an estate of 600 houses at the top of our road. The road took on a different character and we didn't know everybody, even if there were great opportunities for me as an entrepreneur. It was a great place to grow up in, however, and, like all children in those days, we had so much freedom to go out and play.

I moved into my first flat in 1972, when I was working as a trainee manager with Jury's in Sligo. It was my first time living away from a home and I lived in shared staff accommodation. I have to say, as a bit of a neat freak, I was quite shocked at the state of the place. Once, one of my flatmates broke a partition wall; he put a big hole in the side of it and wrecked the bathroom too. I didn't come from a home like that and I was horrified, to be honest. I had been brought up to have respect for other people's belongings, and that included the hotel's, and it never occurred to me not to keep the place neat and tidy. While I was working at the Victoria Hotel in Cork, I went to have a look at a flat in Montenotte. In spite of the posh surroundings, the place wasn't right at all. It was a Georgian house, but there the glamour ended. I fell over about twenty bikes in the hall and I had to go all the way out the back door and through a yard to get to the flat, which was in an old carriage house. I couldn't believe it.

'I have to do this every time I want to get in?' I said to the letting agent, pointing to the bikes.

'Oh, people never take them when they leave,' he explained cheerfully.

I didn't go for that flat, I can assure you! Maybe I wasn't cut out for that kind of thing. In fact, in spite of my sociable nature, I'd say it suits me to live alone, so I can have everything just the way I like it.

When I was general manager at the Park Hotel Kenmare, before I owned the hotel, I rented a chalet in the grounds and then I moved to my existing house near Sneem. I've been here thirty years now. It's a beautiful house, which I've done quite a lot of work to because, when I bought it, it was only a two-up, two-down. I know that it once belonged to an Irish actress who'd gone to Hollywood in the 1930s and had married an actor called Scilacci, who was famous at the time. Details about her were hazy, apart from the fact that she used to come home to Kenmare every so often in her fur coat. When I bought the house in 1985, even though it was quite basic it still had a telephone, which was very exotic, and a well and electricity; it's what we'd call a good Fianna Fáil house! A brother and sister had lived in it last and both had ended up in Bantry Hospital, leaving it pretty much the way it had always been, complete with big open fireplace with hooks in it for the kettle and pot, and a Sacred Heart picture over the mantelpiece. It also had quite a big garden, which I loved doing up. I am a keen gardener, even though I don't really have much time to garden – maybe I can give more time to it in my 'retirement', whenever that happens! I also have the house in Kenmare that featured in *Designs for Life*;

I'll move there in time because it doesn't really have a garden and there'll be no lawn to mow. Grass is a curse when you get old!

Kenmare is also very important to me. I'm never going to leave it because of the people in the community, whom I know so well at this stage. When I first came here, it was a sleepy town, the forerunner of what Kenmare is today – a vibrant, bustling community, with shops and restaurants that offer top-quality food and shopping. I love it – but I'm never home. In the first half of 2015, I was away on a staff holiday plus four days in London in January; then I went away for my US sales trip on 5 February and came back on 21 March; then I was off again in April filming *At Your Service*; and then I was at two conferences in Amsterdam and the Algarve. I finally got home at the beginning of May. I have no goldfish and no houseplants, because they would die when I'm away. I just lock the door and go.

Now, my house might not sound like much of a 'home' to you – considering how little I'm there – but it's very important to me because it's full of memories. Everything I have in my home means something to me: a book I got in Singapore or a stuffed kangaroo somebody gave me in Australia – I was chairman of Small Luxury Hotels of the World for four years and people gave me mementoes of my trips. To me, it's not the house itself that's important. Home means people, and home is Kenmare because that's where everyone is. When I see Kenmare Bay, I think, Oh, I'm home now. It's a sense of place. I don't even have to be meeting and talking to everybody, but I know them all and they know me, and there's Sunday mass, of course. That, to me, is home.

– My rosary beads
and my bottle of holy water –

See below. I always tuck both into my suitcase whenever I'm travelling. I wouldn't be without them.

– The People Who Inspire Me –

Wace Philo – my old hotel manager at the Cheval Roc in Jersey. I always found him inspirational, because he was so organised, being an ex-Navy engineer, and so careful. Nothing ever broke down in the hotel – everything breaks down in the Park Hotel Kenmare before we're even aware anything is wrong, but he always looked after and maintained things so carefully. I learned a lot from him about care and attention to detail. He was also so good to me as a person, never failing to treat me with respect, even though I was only a youngster. I learned so much from him in a short time and he gave me a brilliant grounding in the business. Funnily enough, he never owned his own hotel: he ran the Cheval Roc for many years but never owned it. Maybe he didn't want the responsibility. It's not for everyone.

Denis O'Brien – I find him fantastic. I know that not everyone will agree with me, but I admire the way in which he has assisted so many start-ups in Ireland and has done a lot of work in the background. He was lucky with one deal, but he shares the money around. His top employees worldwide are Irish and he's good to them. And he's always treated so badly in the press. Now, you might think this is fair enough, as he is a public figure, but I imagine every now and again he thinks, Why are they against me? I can't imagine it's easy.

Brendan Maher – Now, you might remember that Brendan was the man who made the staff cry in Parknasilla. He was my first general manager in Ireland. He had been a university graduate who was taken into the hotel industry by the board of the Great Southern; this was rare in the industry at the time, since most people grew up in it, starting when they were just kids and working their way up. But he brought something else to the role – a special quality that was inspiring. He had a difficult streak, but he was a very good organiser. However, I learned most from him in the way he handled guests: he was so proper and professional. And he always told me, 'Never, ever have your tie loose'!

My brother John – John was born twelve years after me, so I didn't know him terribly well as a child. By the time he was going to primary school, I had almost left school altogether and was moving out of home. And, during all the years I was working and in college, he was at home with Mum and Dad and then in school in Sligo. I only really got to know him when he came to work with me at the Park Hotel Kenmare, and he's been such an inspiration to the business. Against adversity, he started a business that has been a great success; he's conquered illness; he's been a great support on *At Your Service*; he has a lovely family; and he juggles all the balls and keeps everybody happy.

The Dalai Lama – I love the Dalai Lama's tranquillity and the way he can communicate his healing and inspiring message around the world. He just brings a spiritual nature to everything he does and everywhere he goes.

Pope John XXIII – I met the pope with my friend Mary Bowe, of Marlfield House Hotel, Co. Wexford, and it was absolutely a highlight for me. We were in Rome for sales calls and Mary had an 'in' with a cardinal, so he arranged for us to go to a private mass said by the pope. There were only eight of us, and afterwards we had breakfast with him and he gave me a pair of rosary beads, which I still treasure. They are the very same pair that I pack with me every time I travel, along with my bottle of holy water, and I take them out every night to say my prayers.

Hillary Clinton – I've always admired people who've had to struggle and Hillary Clinton is someone in that category. She's had to hang on through her husband's political career and then lose out to Obama in the Democratic nomination, and then she had the courage to take on the job of Secretary of State and do it so well. She must be made of steel. Like so many public figures, she invites such criticism and such dislike, as well as admiration and respect. I have a soft spot for hard workers and fighters, and Hillary fits the bill.

– A Special Place –

I'm sure you think I'm going to say Kenmare, but no. I have a little apartment in Majorca and, even though I don't spend a lot of time there, it's very special to me. And the reason for this is that when I arrive there, I know I have no responsibility. It's the one place in the world where I don't have grass to cut, people to supervise, bills to pay, phone calls to make. I go to my apartment and everything is perfect. My trips to the US, which I love, are work, work, work. I have a roster of shows and flights to organise and then I come home – it's never stress free. Filming is great fun, but it can be stressful, and the hotel is full of challenges. In Majorca, I never have to get out of bed, the sun shines most of the time and it's private. Nobody knows me or cares who I am. It's the only place where I can truly relax.

– My happiest memory –

I have so many happy memories – I'm so blessed in this way – but my happiest memory is my mother's eightieth birthday, which we had in Sligo. It was extra special, because we were all there and because it was so good to see her in such good health at eighty. She's still in good health at ninety-three!

So, there you have it, the things in my life that are special to me. Writing them down has reminded me of how important they are to me, and I'd urge you to do the same. I know that some experts recommend keeping a 'gratitude' journal, so that you can jot down all the things you are grateful for every day, and that's a brilliant idea, but, really, if you can just stop and think of one single thing every day that makes you happy or grateful, I think that would be wonderful. I've resolved to do that from now on, as well as to remember some of the other lessons I've learned from writing this book: to live in the moment; to celebrate my friends and family, and the things that matter to me in life; and to keep on going, no matter what. I hope you've enjoyed reading the book and I wish you great happiness.

The End